The making of
WEST SIDE STORY

The making of

WEST SIDE STORY

Keith Garebian

Mosaic Press

OAKVILLE, ON - BUFFALO, NY

Canadian Cataloguing in Publication Data

Garebian, Keith, 1943 -
The making of "West Side Story"
(Classic Broadway musicals)
Includes bibliographical references.

ISBN 0-88962-652-9

I. Bernstein, Leonard, 1918 - 1989. West side story.
I. Title II. Series

ML410.B47G37 1995 782.1'4 C94-930595-2

Published by MOSAIC PRESS, P.O. Box 1032, Oakville, Ontario, L6J 5E9, Canada.
Offices and warehouse at 1252 Speers Road, Units #1&2, Oakville, Ontario, L6L
5N9, Canada and Mosaic Press, 85 River Rock Drive, Suite 202, Buffalo, N.Y.,
14207, USA.

Mosaic Press acknowledges the assistance of the Canada Council and the Dept. of
Canadian Heritage, Government of Canada, for their support of our publishing
programme.

THE CANADA COUNCIL | LE CONSEIL DES ARTS
FOR THE ARTS | DU CANADA
SINCE 1957 | DEPUIS 1957

MOSAIC PRESS, in Canada:
1252 Speers Road, Units #1&2,
Oakville, Ontario, L6L 5N9
Phone / Fax: (905) 825-2130
E-mail:
cp507@freenet.toronto.on.ca

MOSAIC PRESS, in the USA:
85 River Rock Drive, Suite 202,
Buffalo, N.Y., 14207
Phone / Fax: 1-800-387-8992
E-mail:
cp507@freenet.toronto.on.ca

MOSAIC PRESS in the UK and Europe:
DRAKE INTERNATIONAL SERVICES
Market House, Market Place,
Deddington, Oxford. OX15 OSF

TABLE OF CONTENTS

LIST OF ILLUSTRATIONS

for Aunt Pat

Foreword

WEST SIDE STORY was a landmark musical. When it premièred on Broadway in 1957, it showed how dancing, singing, acting, and design could merge into a single means of expression, a seamless unity. Whether it was a completely new vision as a "concept musical," or the pinnacle of an already established tradition, it marked the most impressive body of choreography in a single show, and it was acclaimed as Leonard Bernstein's strongest work for the Broadway stage. There was no overture — only a pantomime with two opposing gangs. The setting was an urban underworld, and the libretto was one of the shortest on Broadway record. And there were obvious parallels to, of all things, Shakespeare's romantic tragedy, *Romeo and Juliet*. It was easy to recognize Tony and Maria as demotic versions of the star-crossed lovers, or to see Paris in Chino, Tybalt in Bernardo, Mercutio in Riff, or Friar Laurence in Doc. But Arthur Laurents' script was also remarkably free in its adaptation of Shakespeare to New York's wild side. It stripped down its own text, even as it concocted a special argot for the Jets, allowing Bernstein and Stephen Sondheim's music and Jerome Robbins' dances to elaborate the story, themes, and moods. Much of the action paralleled Shakespeare's story, but Laurents' subplot (the ill-fated liaison of Bernardo and Anita) ensured that an audience would be involved in the show for over two hours. As Lehman Engel notes in *Words with Music*, "It is the contrapuntal tale of Maria and Tony in *West Side Story* versus Bernardo and Anita that creates a single whole fabric. . . . The balances and contrasts provided by the two couples are incalculably valuable to the whole of *West Side Story*."

It had been uncommon to have a commercial musical end with a hero's death, but street brawls and double deaths suddenly became the very fibre of a Broadway musical. Sure, there were accidental killings and suicides in earlier shows — Billy Bigelow's demise in *Carousel*, and the multiple deaths in *Porgy and Bess*, for instance — but *West Side Story* presented itself as a social play with a tragic ending, and reminded audiences and critics alike about how elusive tragedy had been in Broadway musical tradition.

While not pretending to be an alternative to Shakespeare or to make pedantic points on the nature of tragedy, *West Side Story* sought to be taken seriously. It offered dual plots, both with violent streaks, baseless hatreds, and lurid suspicions. Leonard Bernstein's edgy yet hypnotic score had dark tones and calculated dissonances. The overall theatrical presentation was taut, feverish, yet lyrical. There was a new vitality on the Broadway stage, prompted in part by a theme with contemporary urgency. And there were new faces among the performers, as well as a new attitude toward the Broadway musical.

This book is a stage history of *West Side Story* that chronicles the genesis, evolution, and culmination of the work, and that eventually measures the achievement by standards that fit a particular category. A cathartic musical drama is a far cry from a musical comedy or a revue or an opera. It has its proper place in the Broadway pattern and its fitting public. This book seeks to find that place and to account in some way for the public that responded to the show, which mirrored a significant portion of America in the fifties.

But *West Side Story* prided itself on being an integrated musical — that is, a work in which every element was so well combined with its partners that it was impossible to separate one element from another without damaging the cunning texture. Although the book is usually taken to be the basis of any musical, here words alone had no special significance when divorced from the music or movement. So tightly wrought was the overall piece that it was virtually impossible to guess what had come first — book or music, dance or design. And the reason was simple: the entire production was a total collaboration, in which Robbins, Bernstein, Sondheim, and Laurents worked almost side by side in a rare harmony of egos and temperaments. This is why the structure of my book has a looseness in its middle: in truth, the chapters on design, libretto, and music could be interchanged without altering the book's direction, for while Jerome Robbins will forever have the distinction of having conceived, directed, and choreographed the show, the real process of creation was one in which all the creators nourished one another. There was an artistic generosity on everybody's part, and the result was a work of art where the innovation was a style. Prior to *West Side Story*, most musicals had been staged fairly stodgily, and while it was not the first time the usual conventions had been broken — there had been *Allegro* and *South Pacific* earlier — *West Side Story* represented a major departure from convention.

The impulse to do an integrated work came from all the collaborators. As Robbins explained in *Broadway Song & Story*: "Why did we have to do it separately . . . ? Why did Lenny have to write an opera, Arthur a play, me a ballet? Why couldn't we, in aspiration, try to bring our deepest talents together to the commercial theatre? That was the true *gesture* of the show." And it is precisely in accordance with this gesture that I have not sought to force a rigid order on the evolution of the work.

What my book aims for is some sense of the collaborative excitement, some impressions of the work as it originally played on stage, and some measure of its legacy to Broadway.

Breakthrough Movement Musical

THERE WAS NO OVERTURE before the curtain arose on Oliver Smith's stark, urban-jungle setting, which was a suggestion of city streets, alleyways, and a dark brick wall. Instead, for what Arthur Laurents' script called the Prologue, there was a sharp chord and dissonant finger snapping, guided gradually by a single, piercing orchestral note that ascended in pitch. The opening (as specified in the stage directions) was *"half-danced, half-mimed"* by the loitering gang of Jets who directed their suppressed hostility at their rival gang, the Sharks. Occasional bits of dialogue — really the odd taunting word or phrase — built up the tension. The action, as such, was a dramatic condensation of gang rivalry, with the Jets, led by Riff, swaggering in pride and confidence over their possession of the area. Their arabesques were lyrical, light, easy — effected with little skips and jazz steps mostly on the ball of the foot. Riff's shrugging shoulders denoted both a casual contempt for his enemies and his own easy authority as gang leader. The mood was interrupted by the entrance of Bernardo — dark, handsome, sardonic leader of the Puerto Rican Sharks. He was flicked off, and when he returned with cohorts, he and they were flicked off again with jeers, flashing fists, and more shuffling feet. Movement became celebratory and intimidating, with the finger snapping and arabesques growing jazzier. The Sharks had their own peculiar semaphores — more of a martial body language, with balled-up fists either pulled behind the back or thrust out in a swift karate action.

The stage directions indicated that *"The beginnings of warfare [were] mild at first: a boy being tripped up, or being sandbagged with a flour sack or even being spit on — all with overly elaborate apologies."* This was a stylized but still sinister ritual. Then, with A-rab's mimicry of an airplane in a suddenly deserted area, there was a startling omen: over the wall dropped Bernardo, followed by one Shark after another, until A-rab was totally cut off from escape. Closing in on him, as one of their number stood watching atop the wall, Bernardo made a piercing or cutting gesture at one of his ears. At the lookout's whistle, the Jets tore on, and with the music growing shriller and faster, the choreography broke down into a free-for-all until a police whistle screeched louder and louder, and officers Krupke and Schrank arrived to terminate the battle.

All this took only a few minutes, but so distinctive was the choreography and so expressive the music that it was eloquently clear that the Prologue was a premise for the rest of the drama, and that *West Side Story*, conceived, directed, and choreographed by Jerome Robbins (the first time such a triple duty had been credited to an individual), was (what Richard Kislan calls) a breakthrough "movement-conceived musical" rather than an opera or jukebox entertainment. Never mind that the story was a free adaptation of *Romeo and Juliet* set to the agonies and ecstasies of contemporary gang warfare in New York, or that the script invented a somewhat breezy, deliberately onomatopoeic street argot, or that the highly reputed Leonard Bernstein had composed the music with an unparalleled sense of dramatic subtlety. The dancing was what would tell the story — literally between the lines. The lighting certainly helped, for Robbins had worked a great deal with dance theatre that depended more on lighting than scenery, but the prime focus was on movement — and what a repertoire of movement! It was abundantly clear even from the brief Prologue that the dancing was meant to be assymetrical in a sense, with individual dancers permitted a certain freedom of self-assertion in the matter of arabesques, leaps, pivots, and other body language. Exactness or precise replication of a line or step was not as significant as youthful springiness, grace of carriage, strength in stopping and starting, pausing and releasing. The choreography allowed for differences in emphases and urgency of movement. Within the sequence, we could see the continuity of impulse and the culmination of a dance phrase. When the Jets (white, urban-American street youths) soared in mock-airplane flight, they denoted the thrill of ownership of the street. Their energy was expressive of an innate confidence, a group participation in diversion and danger. The Sharks, on the other hand, danced as intruders, took risks, and forced the issue of territorial possession to a climax of explosive chaos. The gangs were two warring factions, two contrasting Houses of America, and their dance Prologue established the thematic significance of the musical. They were Shakespeare's Capulets and Montagues transferred to another time and place, alike in respective gang pride and similarly mutinous against a rival's authority. Their dance vocabulary was a modern vernacular, using the open position and a compact, self-summarizing image. In this type of show, dance told much of the story, dance revealed character, dance incarnated the tragedy. And it did all this by breaking down the usual boundaries among song, drama, and movement.

Jerome Robbins, however, did not initiate the transformation of the nature, scope, and function of dance in the American musical. In 1936, George Balanchine, trained at the Imperial Ballet School in St. Petersburg and afterwards a member of Serge Diaghilev's Ballets Russes de Monte Carlo, insisted on changing his program credit for *On Your Toes* to read "Choreographed by . . ." rather than the customary "Dances by. . . ." Balanchine's dances in the show were not mere interludes or diversions; they were essential to the plot, which dealt with backstage life in the ballet world. As well as a burlesque of Michel Fokine's ballet *Scheherazade*, Balanchine created a melodramatic jazz ballet called "Slaughter on Tenth Avenue," a satire on gangster stories, in which Ray Bolger began with single taps before proceeding to triple beats and what the *New York Herald Tribune* called "flights of soaring." Unfortunately, audiences did not quite appreciate the sophistication of Balanchine's concept. As George Amberg succinctly phrases it, "Few people realized at the time that the difference between the customary conventional dance arrangement and Balanchine's choreography was not a matter of method but a matter of concept." "Slaughter on Tenth Avenue" carried the plot of *On Your Toes* to a climax, and it was the one episode in the play that never aged. When the musical was revived on Broadway in 1954, Richard Watts, Jr. wrote: "A sizable number of jazz ballets have passed this way since it first appeared, but it still is something of a classic in its field. . . ."

Balanchine went on to choreograph *Babes in Arms* (1937), *Song of Norway* (1944), and *Where's Charley?* (1948) — none of which made dance the most outstanding feature of the show — but his most important contributions remained in neoclassical ballet, particularly for the American Ballet at the Metropolitan Opera. Nevertheless, as Richard Kislan observes, his "work in commercial dance demonstrated the bold and exciting options open to choreographers of show dancing, as well as contributing images and rhythms to his ballets."

Agnes de Mille made the first breakthrough in musicals for ballet as *dramatic narrative*. She had an advantage over Balanchine in that *Oklahoma!* (1943), her breakthrough vehicle, provided a distinctively American idiom with which to revolutionize musical comedy without baffling her audiences. Commissioned to stage the dances because her ballet *Rodeo* (1942) had used American source material in a thoroughly American spirit, de Mille moved a long distance away from ethereal classical ballet, though most of her dancers had classical training. Without the dances, *Oklahoma!* would have been cornily old-fashioned, for (as Gerald Bordman notes in *American Musical Theatre*) the love plot was "a reversion to the standards of long-departed comic opera." The show, however, changed fashions in musicals for two decades. Agnes de Mille choreographed the dances to advance the action of the story. In Kislan's words: "her dancers appeared as characters in the show and not merely impersonal instruments for dance entertainment. . . ." To the vigorous and robust dynamic quality of the dances, de Mille "harnessed a ballet-oriented movement mode characterized by open body positions and generous extensions that evoked a feeling of endless space and air." The dream ballet, "Laurie Makes Up Her Mind," in which Jud violently interrupts Laurie's imminent marriage to Curly, was not an interpolation or a special show-piece for stopping the show with claptrap dancing. It was an integral part of the action. Although it is not really Laurie who dances in the dream, but her alter ego, it is the real Laurie who awakens with her fear of Jud brought home to her.

De Mille's counterpart was Jack Cole, a specialist in hybrid exotica. Noted for his choreography of *Alive and Kicking* (1950), which mixed African, Hindu, and other movements, and *Kismet* (1953), which furthered his interest in Orientalia and bent-knee positions, Cole showed that his forté was dance that startlingly reversed direction with ferocious energy. One of his dancers, Florence Lessing, recalls in *Hoofing on Broadway* that "It [was] extremely difficult to master. So many parts of the body, so many muscles moving in opposition to each other, and in isolation from the other!" Yet, despite this technical challenge, his dances were full of emotion.

After people such as de Mille, Cole, and Balanchine, the American musical was compelled to make way for the choreographer-director who could run the whole show. Kislan reports that while "the dance directors brought each new project a well-worn little black book of routine steps" so that audiences might forget about the story for awhile and applaud the choreography, the choreographer-director was responsible for the entire show. It was simply inadequate to be a revisionist Busby Berkeley or John Tiller or Ned Wayburn. Even to be a modern Seymour Felix or Albertina Rasch or Robert Alton was not enough. Bright, sexy, joyful dancing unencumbered by serious purpose, symbolic meaning, or organic connection to plot was anathema to more knowing audiences, who wanted dance to be a kinetic commentary on a story, theme, or character. Where dance directors worked for audience approval, choreographers worked for audience enlightenment.

This new spirit of dance yielded new forms. The style of a dance became the visual symbol of a mode of thought. What Laurie was feeling and thinking was expressed by de Mille's dream ballet, just as what the Jets and Sharks thought of territory and their own identities became inseparable from their movements. With Jerome Robbins, dance was synonymous with emotion and thought, and so the amplification of dance by the integration of song, music, speech, and pantomime became an amplification of drama. Ballet in a musical could also become far more intimate than it had been before, for, under Balanchine, de Mille, and Robbins, ballet evolved an elaborate vocabulary of movement particularly conceived for and suited to the visual presentation of psychological themes and conflicts.

Robbins extended American idioms and images to encompass indigenous training, experience, and environment. He showed in *Fancy Free* (1944), in which he danced himself, that contemporary American idioms could be eloquent without being pretentious, spontaneous and frank without being unduly aggressive, and theatrical without being untrue. *Fancy Free* was a one-act ballet about three sailors on shore leave during World War II. It had a comic veneer with strut, noise, and flash. The three sailors in a bar were competitive and full of ploys, with one always forced to be the odd-man-out. He would have to pay for the beer and be without a gal once the gamesmanship was all over, but, by the luck of things, the three women of the piece could not make up their minds, which provoked a brawl among the three men. Things got so rough that the women stomped out, leaving the men to make amends to one another and resume their old friendship.

The ballet began explosively with a jolly, rollicking bang, but there were wonderful transitions and modulations to slower, relaxed moods, phases of dreamy waiting, with sudden changes of tempo. Hot boogie-woogie turned to slow, torchy blues, but the work was free from sentimentality, and it had a casualness that was deceptive: the choreography was intelligible and precisely suited to every character. Each sailor was given a solo. Each dance was brilliant enough to be showy, yet individualistic enough to project a distinct personality. And there was an overall meaning to all the dancing, beyond the bar manners, random flirtations, and intense competitiveness. According to George Amberg, the true significance of the ballet was "the revelation of democratic human relationships." The six fancy-free young people (the sailors and their gals) were united by a similarity of spirit and feeling. Under their "rough and tumble exterior" there was "a real affection for each other," as Robbins himself noted in his libretto. "Here, at last," Winthrop Palmer remarks in his book on theatrical dancing in America, "was a real American ballet, rich with the great traditions of great dancing." Robbins had obviously learned and "made part of himself" the colour and style of Russian dancing and the "lyric restraint of

English ballet," but *Fancy Free* had more than these qualities: "it had the pace of America and the droll swagger and wit of Americans who, whether soldier, sailor, tinker, tailor, rich man, poor man, beggarman or thief, enjoy a laugh at their own expense." Preeminent dance critic Edwin Denby called the ballet "a very remarkable comedy piece," for he found its pantomime and dances "witty, exuberant" and "natural," and he applauded its "direct, manly" character, which didn't have "any of that coy showing off of 'folk' material." In fact, he judged it to be "as sound as a superb vaudeville turn; in ballet terminology it is perfect American character ballet."

Fancy Free allied three figures for the first time: Robbins, composer Leonard Bernstein, and designer Oliver Smith. They would collaborate again on *Facsimile* (1946), which Amberg calls "Robbins' first and only excursion into the realm of psychology," a collection of variations which paraphrased "emotional impotence, morbid frustration, neurotic exhibitionism and empty social sophistication." An earnest satire of a flirtation between an idle woman and two idle men, it portrayed an awkward triangular tangle which grew heated and hysterical until the woman stopped the frenzy with a cry, and the characters subsided into politeness, humiliation, and emptiness. Edwin Denby provided an acute critique: "To pretend to be sexy is a farce situation and Robbins hasn't missed the jokes. But he has given his characters a spasmodic groping drive that indicates they are passionately pretentious. The devouring drive of vainglory is a tragic subject. But *Facsimile* doesn't go that far. Its characters stop prematurely; after the embarrassing cry there is no further development, no shock of terror, no fury, disintegration or resolution." Yet, despite calling the ending "pathetically trivial," Denby praised the craftsmanship — the "cartoonist wit," the unbroken continuity made up of "fragmentary, often constricted gestures," the bold rhythm, and the long main climax.

Prior to his work as choreographer, Robbins had been a ballet dancer with a varied and interesting background. Born in New York City on October 11, 1918, he grew up in New Jersey. He was always interested in the theatre — particularly in puppetry — and after a year's work in chemistry at New York University (he dropped out because of lack of funds), he became interested in dance. His sister, Sonya, was a dance instructor, and she guided him to teachers such as Antony Tudor, Eugene Loring, Ella Daganova, and Helene Platova. His training was eclectic: New Dance, Oriental, Modern Interpretive. He also studied piano, violin, and acting. His first significant experience was as a member of the Glück Sandor-Felicia Sorel Dance Center, New York, in 1938, where he participated in studio performances. He also worked briefly with the Yiddish Art Theatre and was hired by Max Liebman to do his first choreography for small shows and revues. Robbins found additional employment in Broadway choruses for shows such as *Great Lady* (1938), *Stars in Your Eyes* (1939), *Straw Hat Revue* (1939), and *Keep Off the Grass* (1940).

In 1940, Robbins joined the Ballet Theatre, founded that year by Lucia Chase and Richard Pleasant. Formed in order to present all kinds of ballet, from the Russian classics and the Diaghilev repertory to contemporary American works, Ballet Theatre engaged some of the greatest choreographers and ballet stars of the past thirty years — such as Anton Dolin, Antony Tudor, David Lichine, Leonide Massine, Agnes de Mille, George Balanchine, Bronislava Nijinska, Michel Fokine in the first case, and Erik Bruhn, Alicia Alonso, Alicia Markova, Nora Kaye, Rosella Hightower, Maria Karnilova, and Tamara Toumanova in the second. Robbins quickly distinguished himself in *Pillar of Fire* (1942), de Mille's *Three Virgins and a Devil* (a satire on virginal vanity), *Capriccio Espagnol*, and David Lichine's weakly choreographed *Helen of Troy* — the last three all in 1943. At the very first performance of *Three Virgins and a Devil*, he stole the show in a walk-on part. Sono Osato, who partnered him in several of the ballets, recalls in her autobiography how his audacious sense of humour shone on stage. "In one passage Jerry walked jauntily to center stage and paused to admire one of the virgins, while twirling a flower nonchalantly in his hand. He gave the chaste girl a knowing nod, tipped his hat, and sauntered offstage again with a bobbing gait. With just those few gestures he never failed to make an audience chuckle or titter with glee." Edwin Denby noted of *Helen* (in *Dance Writings*) that "Jerome Robbins, as Mercury, has of course the most original part, and he does it beautifully. . . . So Robbins, on the stage, by being very natural, looks different enough to be a god. . . ." In other character roles, he showed admirable attack, and though his technique was faulted in *Petrouchka* (1943) for falling short in the realization of character and story, he was recognized for his remarkable talent and originality. Denby praised his "poetic love for the air of rudeness and unresponsiveness in [American] national manners."

In 1949 Robbins joined the New York City Ballet (run by Balanchine and Lincoln Kirstein) where, during his first ten-year stint with the company, he devised nine ballets, including *The Cage* (1951), an insect-inspired allegory; a modern version of *Afternoon of a Faun* (1953); and *The Concert* (1956), a comic ballet about an onstage concert by a pretentious pianist before a farcical audience. He also danced the title role in Balanchine's *The Prodigal Son* (1950). His pieces of choreography and his own dance were obviously benchmarks of a laboratory process that produced extraordinary results. His choreography was exceptional in that it was unrepetitive, disciplined, and driving. Edwin Denby found "the dramatic pressure" of *The Cage* to be "extraordinary," because it devoured the notes and forced the gesture. *Faun*, set in a dance studio and using only two dancers, had a quietly intimate, psychological focus, yet one that was highly dramatic. It was a tentative love duet for a pair who encountered each other in a rehearsal place and who related by first watching themselves in the (invisible) mirror. *The Concert* showed that Robbins could be as successfully comic as he could be dramatic. The characters were stock types: a hen-pecked, cigar-chomping husband and his domineering wife; a dithery blond; a belligerent female student; a young bespectacled male wimp; and a pair of noisy young women who disturbed the concert with their chatter and cellophane-wrapped sweets. The dances ranged from an unsynchronized sextet of ballerinas to a Russian folk dance with allegorical butterflies and moths.

Because of his eclectic training in dance, it was, perhaps, inevitable that Robbins would become interested in Broadway musicals. What was less inevitable was the degree of his success in the genre. When *On the Town* premièred in 1944, Edwin Denby wrote: "You can tell what an exceptional gift he has as a director by how clearly the dancers know what to stress and how spontaneously they do it." Robbins' skill with the ensemble and his genius with infusing the dances with an intelligent unselfconsciousness especially appealed to the critic: "There are lots and all sizes of dances; they generally tell a little pantomime story, but you don't think of them as distinct from the rest of the show. They generally emerge from the stage action and melt into it again so as to give value to a scene rather than a hand to the dance. Often they express a sentiment, too, much as Miss de Mille's musical comedy dances do." The dances did not have very "complicated patterns" or "ornamental gestures." Instead, they had "clarity of impulse" and "variety of pacing."

Essentially an expansion of the *Fancy Free* ballet, *On the Town* told the story of three sailors on a twenty-four-hour leave in New York. The sailors were stock types and foils to one another: a romantic (Gaby), a clown (Ozzie), and an earthbound lover (Chip). Leonard Bernstein's score was lively, contemporary, and often hot — especially when the spirit of Manhattan was used to jazz up the tempo.

Billion Dollar Baby (1945) was next — "a brash and not altogether feeling or faithful look at the bygone twenties," according to Bordman — and reunited him with Betty Comden and Adolph Green, who had written the lyrics for *On the Town*. Robbins did extensive research in the atmosphere of the 1920s, and provided the Charleston and dance marathon that highlighted the show. Unfortunately, the ersatz twenties quality did not suit the times, and the show was lucky to last seven months.

But Robbins was luckier with *High Button Shoes* (1947), a conventional musical comedy set in 1913, in New Brunswick, New Jersey. It told the story of a bungling small time con man. The book was not especially witty, but Phil Silvers' rambunctious clowning as the con man amused audiences. Nanette Fabray and Jack McCauley also had their share of notice as they performed Jule Styne's foot-stomping polka, "Papa, Won't You Dance With Me?" and the sentimental soft-shoe "I Still Get Jealous." But the highlight was Robbins' wild Mack Sennett Ballet, in which Silvers and his crony were chased by the villagers, bathers, Keystone Kops, and a bear, as an ensemble ran around with tambourines and did knee drops to the "Second

Hungarian Rhapsody." Audiences of 1500 would stand up and yell "Bravo!" at the sheer delightful absurdity. For his choreographic pains, Robbins was given a Donaldson Award and a Tony.

Two more Donaldsons were to come with *The King and I* (1951) and *Two's Company* (1952). In the first, Robbins was rather long winded, but his skill with blending the sentimental operetta tradition with Orientalia and musical comedy was undeniably spectacular. His ballet, "The Small House of Uncle Thomas," revealed an outstanding interaction between historical information and artistic creativity. Kislan describes how this ballet, based on Harriet Beecher Stowe's *Uncle Tom's Cabin*, grew out of a "determination to focus attention on the evils of slavery. . . . Robbins borrowed idioms from the oriental theater like mime, masks, stylized movement, and stylized gesture and then put them to the service of a functional dance entertainment that remains even today as one of the glories of the American musical theater." When the show was revived in 1977, Richard Philp wrote in *Dance Magazine* of how "men dressed in black and kneeling on the floor become mountains; women holding branches become the forest. Simon Legree, dressed in the devil's costume, pursues the fleeing Eliza with a walk in which his arms and legs are exaggeratedly turned out. . . . The Angel from Buddha, Eliza's protector, conveys the feeling of a benediction through gracefully turning hands. . . ." By contrast, *Two's Company* was definitely flat and uninteresting, though its lyrics were written by Ogden Nash and its music by Vernon Duke. With an unmusical performance by Bette Davis, it ran for a mere ninety performances and wonder was that Robbins emerged unscathed.

Peter Pan (1954) extended Robbins' versatility, for it revealed a master of childlike fantasy. Technically, it was not a difficult show for dancing, but Robbins turned a ballet with lion and ostrich in Never Land into an enchanting fantasia and, by putting a fireman's pole into Peter Pan's abode, and a flying harness onto Mary Martin, was able to exploit comedy, tempo, and romantic wish fulfillment. A television version of this production won Robbins an Emmy to add to his *Dance Magazine* Award in 1950 for a performance in Balanchine's *The Prodigal Son*.

Even to this point, Robbins' career showed resourcefulness, an indigenous vitality and sense of humour, a concise storytelling power, and an obsession with rhythm. Robbins appeared to have an instinctive understanding of the formal unity of a ballet in stage space and musical time, and his dance impetus was always coherent. No doubt, his growing involvement with the Broadway musical was disconcerting to critics, such as Edwin Denby, who did not want him to reduce his experiments with American ballet, but Robbins could well have countered with the claim that the Broadway musical has standards of serious artistry, is committed to dance as an expressive medium, and encourages expansion of various modes of movement. Indeed, with the influx of ballet and modern choreographers into the musical theatre, dancers are required to have a higher level of proficiency than ever before, and the choreography has become more complex than (as Winthrop Palmer notes) "the precision dancing and 'routines' of earlier years." Dance has "acquired more importance in the general scheme of the musical play," and choreographers have benefited in turn, for their works have been introduced to a wider audience.

Today, after Bob Fosse, Michael Bennett, Gower Champion, Tommy Tune, and Michael Kidd, the importance and contribution of the choreographer-director are beyond dispute, but we should not forget that it was Jerome Robbins who first conceived of and executed an entire musical as a dance-drama. As the brief prologue of *West Side Story* demonstrated, the dance form was, indeed, the content. And (as Richard Kislan phrases it) "[w]hoever controlled the movement controlled the show."

Genesis

LEONARD BERNSTEIN became one of the greatest conductors of his time, with only fragile ties to European culture but with an enthusiastic appreciation of American jazz. Born to immigrant Jewish parents, Sam and Jennie Bernstein, in Boston on August 25, 1918, he seemed to have a life filled with schizophrenic dualities. His legal name was "Louis" rather than "Leonard," but because his parents preferred the latter, he never knew his own legal name for his first five years. This early confusion was a prelude of sorts to his eventual anomalies. He came to be torn between composing and conducting, between art music and pop, between heterosexuality and bisexuality. But whatever his inner confusions, he had undeniable genius. His mother claimed that "when he was about four or five, he would play an imaginary piano on his windowsill. When he finally got a piano, he . . . made love to it all the time." He would play late at night and disturb his father's sleep, but Sam, a very successful businessman with an orthodox religious sense, realized his son's musical seriousness. At an anniversary party for a rabbi, young Bernstein took a melody from the High Holy Day music he had heard his father sing in the shower, and played it in the styles of Mozart, Chopin, and Gershwin. With his prodigious gift for sight reading, he could take any score and master it with ease. At fifteen, he played the Grieg Piano Concerto; at college he played with the Massachusetts State Symphony.

The seeds for his eventual involvement in Broadway musicals were planted early in his adolescence. At fourteen, he staged an Americanized version of *Carmen*, written in collaboration with classmate Dana Schnittkind, and with boys playing girls and vice versa. "The score was much simplified," he explained to his biographer, Joan

Peyser, "with lots of cuts, and our version of the libretto was full of private jokes and allusions to Sharon [Massachusetts]." Two summers later, his group (calling itself the Sharon Community Players) staged *The Mikado* (in which he played Nanki-Poo), and then *H.M.S. Pinafore* the following year. But the centre of his teen life was really jazz. At parties he would play jazz, standing with his coat open so that he could go on to another party and play some more. George Gershwin was a particular favourite. Bernstein studied music first with Helen Coates and then with Heinrich Gebhard, and his academic education was also élitist, for he attended Boston Latin School, which had been founded in 1635, with an alumni roster that included Cotton Mather, John Hancock, Ralph Waldo Emerson, George Santayana, and Bernard Berenson. Here he took six years of Latin, four of French, and two of German, as well as the usual range of history, English, and mathematics. He also attended Hebrew school every afternoon after class. This rich mixture of religion, the classics, and music produced a well-rounded graduate, who excelled in the glee club even as he scooped up awards for the classics, reading, and moderns.

At Harvard, he followed the pattern established at Boston Latin. He was brilliantly eclectic, but a little too diverse. He studied composition and theory with Walter Piston, a distinguished American composer, but did not spend enough time on assignments. He was always putting on a show or playing piano accompaniment for classic silent movies at the Harvard Film Society. He also began to write impudent but perceptive music criticism for both the *Harvard Advocate*, where he was music editor, and *Modern Music*, an influential New York journal devoted to contemporary music. In January, 1937, he met Dimitri Mitropoulos, a brilliant Greek conductor, who afforded him an intoxicating tutelage in conducting. In his senior year, he composed incidental music (with, as Joan Peyser writes, "exotic themes, strange rhythms, and new harmonies, particularly those from Far Eastern sources") for a production of Aristophanes' *The Birds*, presented by the Classical Club. Six weeks later, on May 27, 1939, he staged, directed, and played piano at the Sanders Theater for Marc Blitzstein's *The Cradle Will Rock*, a play about unionism. He performed the entire score from memory, and this production (in which his younger sister Shirley played a prostitute) showed a remarkable convergence of politics and aesthetics — something that would be repeated to various degrees in his own operas years later.

Bernstein's interest in vernacular words and music fed into his 1939 Bachelor's thesis (reprinted in *Findings*), which analyzed various "racial codes" that comprised the essence of American music. Entitled "The Absorption of Race Elements into American Music," it defined a new and vital American nationalism as something "organic," something that had grown in two stages — the first being a "material" one in which actual folk material was used simply as folk material, and the second being "spiritual," where folk material permeated "the whole of a composition, so that the entire piece sounded typical of the country." Discoursing on American social and cultural history, Bernstein argued that pioneer America had "no fundamental racial unit," and so "no *common* American musical material." However, in the twentieth century, there were two common racial musical elements — the first being "the music of the New England colonists, which includ[ed] the hymn or Protestant chorale, with its American modifications, and the wealth of English, Irish, and Scottish folk music"; and the second being the jazz influence of the Negroes, with its eventual combinations with Spanish, Latin American, and French music, or with Protestant hymn singing and the mountain music of Tennessee. The thesis concluded that the most important phenomenon in twentieth-century American music is jazz (especially that of Gershwin and Copland), which has entered the mind and spirit of America, "and if an American is a sensitive creator, jazz will have become an integral part of his palette, whether or not he is aware of it."

Until he met the great European conductor Serge Koussevitzky, Bernstein did not subscribe to generalizations about "high" and "low" art. Whereas purists asserted that the roots of formal ("high") art lay in Europe and that American forms were inescapably vulgar, Bernstein was not engaged by this argument. His own formal music education was begun late and his family ties to European culture were fragile, so he never avoided American models or popular forms.

After Gershwin, he annexed Aaron Copland as his trademark, becoming a personal friend of the composer, conducting *Billy the Kid*, *Appalachian Spring*, *El Salón México*, the Piano Sonata, and film scores to *Quiet City*, *Of Mice and Men*, and *Our Town*.

He composed his first large-scale serious work, *Jeremiah*, for a competition sponsored by the New England Conservatory of Music (where the principal judge was his mentor, Koussevitzky), but he lost to Gardner Read, a conservative composer. Perhaps the judges disliked the popular aspect of Bernstein's gifts, unlike the critics who bestowed the 1943–44 Music Critics Circle Award on the piece. The young composer became Artur Rodzinski's assistant conductor for the New York Philharmonic in 1943, and then leaped to glory when he took over the orchestra for a concert that Bruno Walter was too ill to conduct. He was suddenly in great demand as a guest conductor, and he eagerly accepted all invitations.

Bernstein fell under the spells of Fritz Reiner and Serge Koussevitzky. From classes on conducting offered by Reiner at the Curtis Institute in Philadelphia, he learned the highest standards of musicology and conducting; from Koussevitzky, a warm, inviting theatricality to go along with the dramatic approach acquired from Mitropoulos. But his interests were eclectic. He followed modern ballet and dance eagerly. In October, 1943, a dancer named Jerome Robbins asked him if he could write a ballet score, and described his own idea for *Fancy Free*. The young composer devised a jazz score that was perfect for the aggressive "urban sexuality" of the piece, and conducted the work with what *The New Yorker*'s Robert Simon called "an almost pugnacious direction." Bernstein was fêted, along with Robbins, for having created the finest ballet on an American theme. But Serge Koussevitzky regarded *Fancy Free* as a threat to his control over his protegé. To the older man's horror, the ballet was expanded into a highly successful Broadway musical, *On the Town*, and Koussevitzky spent many hours berating Bernstein for wasting his time on this show, and attempting to lure his devotee away from it by giving him assignments to conduct Sibelius, Tchaikovsky, and Ravel. Koussevitzky reluctantly attended the Boston opening of *On the Town* (1944) and muttered patronizingly: "Good boy, Lenushka, it is a noble jezz." But even as his protegé won great critical and popular favour for his score, Koussevitzky did not relent in his attempt to liberate him. After the Broadway opening, the master felt let down and declared: "You must choose. You can not have everything. All that musical talent, all that excitement, all that brain going to waste!" Indeed, in the closing years of the forties, Koussevitzky forbade Bernstein to compose for Broadway, directing him to inhibit his theatrical flair and to confine his jazz in art works. Koussevitzky's artistic credo was marked by a sense of social responsibility. Peyser reports that, at the Berkshire Music Center, which he founded in 1940 in Tanglewood, Massachusetts, he declared: "You must conduct your lives in such a way, that when you come out on the stage to lead your orchestra, you can truthfully say to yourself: 'Yes, I have the right to appear before these lovers of good music. They can watch me without shame. I have the right because my life and work are clean.'"

Bernstein yielded a little to his teacher's will, though he never scorned the Broadway musical. In November, 1954, he composed an imaginary exchange of documents between himself (L.B.) and an anonymous Broadway Producer (B.P.) which amounted to an argument in favour of an American musical language in the theatre. A witty piece, entitled "Whatever Happened To That Great American Symphony?" (published in *The Joy of Music*), it really projected his own convictions, buttressed by a knowledge of musical history and coloured by his passion for contemporary American music. L.B. allowed himself to be wooed by B.P.'s "theory" of music, which saw the origins of music in "folklore, comprising songs and dances of prayer, of work, of celebration, of love." This meant that music was first attached to words and ideas. B.P.'s argument encompassed a quick set of examples in which the symphony was shown to have derived from the opera overture (as with Mozart), and in which preludes and fugues were seen to be "reverie-pieces" used in church services (as in Bach). In short, European audiences had grown up with music in theatrical form before ever being able to relate to music *without* the theatre. Consequently, it was argued that American musical language must first be created in the theatre before it could divorce itself from "meaning" and stand alone as something abstract. Americans had their own folk music in jazz, and out of it had come something called "the musical comedy," and "the real pieces of importance and interest to America now [were] not X's Fourteenth Symphony and Y's Flute Soliloquy, but *Finian's Rainbow* and *Carousel* and maybe even *Wonderful Town* and *South Pacific."*

In a subsequent piece, "The World of Jazz," an *Omnibus* television program telecast on October 16, 1955, Bernstein exhibited his admiration for jazz and strengthened his claim that "all music has low-class origins, since it comes from folk music, which is necessarily earthy." This must have made some purists blush, but Bernstein was always against dullness and pretentious solemnity. He raised controversy when he declared in a newspaper interview that he always did what seemed like fun at the time. In *Findings* he reports that he was promptly upbraided for his "light attitude toward music and for [his] apparent lack of social responsibility in giving [his] art serious thought," but he rebutted these criticisms in an article which listed "sense of rightness," "tranquillity," "balance," "catharsis," "expressivity," "participation," "creativity," "order," "sublimation," and "energy release" as integral elements of fun. He asserted: "Fun is the 'x' of the equation that tries to solve the riddle of why art exists at all."

His prodigious success as a conductor left him little or no time for theatre work. But when Jerome Robbins called him on January 6, 1949, with an idea for a contemporary Romeo and Juliet story set to music, he was excited by the idea of a Shakespearean adaptation. In *Broadway Song & Story*, Robbins tells how he was approached by an actor-friend who had just been offered the role of Romeo. "This part seems very passive," the friend complained. "Would you tell me what you think I should do with it?" Robbins wondered to himself: "If I were to play this, how would I make it come to life?" He was struck by "the intensity of adolescent feeling in the play," and began to think of "how to transpose this violence of emotion to the world today." During his search for contemporary analogies, something clicked in his mind. So he wrote a very brief outline and started looking for a producer and collaborators who would be interested.

This was no easy task, for producers were not terribly excited by the idea of a Romeo and Juliet story set in contemporary New York. As for collaborators, he recruited Arthur Laurents for the libretto and made a pitch for Bernstein to compose the score. Bernstein's diary entry (quoted by Joan Peyser) records the occasion:

Jerry R. called today with a noble idea: a modern version of *Romeo and Juliet* set in the slums at the coincidence of Easter-Passover celebrations. Feelings run high between Jews and Catholics. Former: Capulets; latter: Montagues. Juliet is Jewish. Friar Laurence is a neighborhood druggist. Street brawls, double death — it all fits. But it's all much less important than the bigger idea of making a musical that tells a tragic story in musical-comedy terms, using only musical-comedy techniques, never falling into the 'operatic' trap. Can it succeed? It hasn't yet in our country.

Four evenings later, Bernstein caught up with Arthur Laurents at Robbins' apartment. "I remember that evening in Jerry's apartment as though it were yesterday *because* of the excitement," recalled Bernstein in *Broadway Song & Story*. "What was basically different from the way *West Side Story* turned out was that it was conceived as taking place on the *East* side of New York." Robbins' original idea was to use Shakespeare's play in order to tell a story of feuding Catholics and Jews at Passover time, when feelings ran very high in the streets and there were real prospects of brawls and blood letting. It seemed to Bernstein to match the Romeo story very well, "except that this was not a family feud, but religion-oriented."

According to Bernstein, Laurents displayed "a sudden outburst of hostility. . . . He announced vehemently, 'I want to make one thing clear before we go any further, and that is that I'm not writing any fucking libretto for any goddamned Bernstein opera!' " Bernstein was a little surprised. After all, the two men had only just met, even though each had been quite aware of the other's solid achievements. Bernstein acknowledges in *Sondheim & Co.* that he did understand what Laurents was talking about, "since *Aida*, *Falstaff*, and *Otello* are known as Verdi operas," despite the fact that their libretti have a great deal to do with their success and beauty. "Since he knew I was a serious composer and that the show might have operatic overtones — or might even turn out to be an opera — he wasn't going to get lost on the way. I pacified him and tried to make it clear that I considered him as important as any of us, more so in fact, because we were utterly dependent on what he would do."

After this meeting, Bernstein and Laurents began their respective work on the score and book. Laurents wrote some sketched-out scenes, only one of which was complete, and Bernstein, who was then in St. Louis, Missouri, conducting the orchestra, was thrilled when he received the playwright's opening scene and an outline of the second. But after a few more pages of the libretto, both men sensed that something was deadly wrong. By his own account (in *Sondheim & Co.*), Bernstein had "a strong feeling of staleness of the East Side situation" and did not like "the too-angry, too-bitchy, too-vulgar tone." Both men recognized that the East Side wasn't what it used to be: there had been an influx of Latin Americans, and the Jewish-Catholic ghettoes were not now the exclusive zones of gang rivalry. Therefore, the basic idea was old-fashioned, a sort of warmed-over *Abie's Irish Rose* and, so, not very topical. The title changed from *East Side Story* to *Gangway!*, but this was no help at all. Ballerina Nora Kaye jibed at Laurents: " '*Abie's Irish Rose*' to music. The dance of the garbage cans." But garbage-can naturalism was the last thing any of the collaborators wanted to see in the theatre, particularly the musical theatre, for their collective hope was to make the stage more theatrical, more lyrical, more magically exciting. As Laurents recalled, he, Robbins, and Bernstein talked of the balcony scene played on "a gossamer fire escape; the language lifted above modern street level until it soared into song at the moment the lovers first kissed. And at that moment the surrounding buildings would disappear, leaving the lovers in space, in their own world." Nora Kaye liked this notion and others as well, but she predicted cheerfully, "Nevertheless, you'll never write it. Your three temperaments in one room, and the walls will come down."

By April of the same year, Bernstein was on a lengthy conducting tour while Laurents commuted between New York and Hollywood. Bernstein realized that "this remote-control collaboration" wasn't right and thought it better if Robbins and Laurents could find a composer who wasn't "always skipping off to conduct somewhere." Serge Koussevitzky was still a large presence in his life. According to Peyser, "he and Bernstein spent summers at Tanglewood, probably with the mutual understanding that . . . Bernstein would one day take over his mentor's orchestra. Bernstein was also committed to a U.S. tour" with the Israeli orchestra, sharing the directing duties with "Koussy." So it was inevitable that for the time being he would turn down any further offers to work on Robbins' project.

After his tour with the Israeli Philharmonic, Bernstein rented a house in Guernavaca in order to work on his next creation. The piece (called an opera, probably to appease Koussevitzky) was *Trouble in Tahiti*, a satire about an unhappy suburban couple. Jazz and popular song were used to create what Bernstein called "a lightweight piece," with roots in "musical comedy, or, even better, the American musical theater." The work premièred at the Brandeis festival (where Bernstein served as consultant) in June, 1952, along with Marc Blitzstein's translation and adaptation of Kurt Weill's *Threepenny Opera*. Reviews were mixed, with several critics unable to appreciate the beauty of the main theme and the long stretch of operatic music that ends the work. However, Harold Taubman recognized Bernstein's "delicious and irresistible vitality," and Irving Kolodin described the score as "crisp and flavorsome, even witty."

In November, 1952, NBC produced a television version of *Trouble in Tahiti*, using a different cast from the one at Brandeis, and improving on the original in some ways. Bernstein dedicated the piece to Marc Blitzstein, who had helped him solve problems in the libretto. The irony of this work and its official dedication was not lost on Bernstein's friends and colleagues: the opera about a disintegrating marriage had been written while its composer was on his honeymoon, yet the dedication had gone not to his wife but to a male friend.

Meanwhile, the Broadway musical was moving toward new peaks without Bernstein. Koussevitzky had died in 1951, and Bernstein no longer had to worry about his disapproval. He was free to write again for Broadway, but his next musical was *Wonderful Town*, an adaptation of *My Sister Eileen*, with book by Joseph Fields and Jerome Chodorov, lyrics by Betty Comden and Adolph Green, choreography by Donald Saddler, and direction by George Abbott. According to Stanley Green (in *The World of Musical Comedy*), neither Comden nor Green was enthusiastic about the show because *My Sister Eileen*, their source material, had seemed (according to Green) "so awfully Thirties-bound, sort of a post-Depression play, full of overexploited plot lines and passé references." Bernstein, however, was excited: "The Thirties! My God, those were the years! The excitement that was around! The political awareness! F.D.R.! Fiorello! Real personalities! And the wonderful fashions! Glorious! And the songs! What beat!" Rarely has a composer gushed with such force, but Bernstein matched his creativity to his enthusiasm. All his numbers reflected the pace and spirit of New York in the mid-thirties, and they expressed a wealth of sophisticated devices, creating tunes that adroitly repeated motifs and that were not merely memorable but integral parts of the story. Rosalind Russell starred in the show, which set a house record during its first week of previews in Boston. Robbins managed to be a part of the show when he was called in to help with the dances. The Broadway opening on February 25, 1953, received eight favourable reviews, all of which pointed to the excellence of the score. Peyser's praise is typical: "Bernstein showed how he could combine the vernacular with sophisticated techniques, and use jagged, offbeat meters and distinctive Bernstein dissonances to give a hard edge to a popular sound." Olin Downes wrote in the *New York Times* that the show was so "utterly American in conception and execution" that it was "not paralleled by any other musical theater, for better or worse, of the contemporaneous world." Downes added: "This is an opera of which dance is warp and woof, an opera made of dance, prattle and song and speed. Its unflagging pulse is characteristic of its restless time and nervous environment." Bernstein's score (written in less than five weeks) was appreciated by critics and audiences for being what Joan Peyser calls "an effervescent tone poem in praise of New York." Bernstein had temporarily put aside Copland and Stravinsky in favour of older styles and sounds — some right out of Brahms!

Three years later, Bernstein became involved in a Broadway project apparently designed to ridicule what is normally thought of as "high" art. Even as he was destined for a pre- eminent position as a "classical" conductor in 1956, Bernstein began work on *Candide*, a sophisticated parody of opera. He aimed at changing American music, for he believed that the Broadway musical as a genre would eventually lead to the appreciation of serious American music. Michael Freedland quotes Bernstein: "The best music always follows a theatre period. It grows up in the theatre. Once a musical idea is firmly established, it starts in the theatre, the public hears it and from then on it can be detached from its theatrical form."

Voltaire's satire seemed particularly appropriate to Bernstein, for he saw in the work matters of (what he called) "puritanical snobbery, phony moralism, inquisitory attacks on the individual, brave-new-world optimism, essential superiority" which were of topical relevance in America. The problem, however, was that his lilting score and the lyrics credited to Richard Wilbur, John Latouche, and Dorothy Parker did not jell with Lillian Hellman's dark libretto. Hellman's book was vigorously explicit and humanitarian rather than ironic and diabolic as Voltaire's writing had been, and Bernstein's score, as Richard Wilbur remarked, "got more and more pretentious and smashy and conducive to amnesia — the audience forgot what was happening to the characters." An astute critic complained that the score was a "gay pastiche of past styles and forms," with something akin to Gilbert and Sullivan spoofing, duets, quartet finales, gavottes, tangos, mazurkas, *schottisches* and waltzes that could be danced.

Yet, as he was satirizing and parodying opera in *Candide*, Bernstein came to a vital realization: the more a Broadway show moved away from pure diversion, the closer it moved toward opera. Paradoxically, he was parodying the very thing that purists considered "high" art. This battle between "low" Broadway *divertissement* and "high" classical seriousness was to flare again with *West Side Story*. He recorded in his diary: "*Candide* is on again. . . . So again *Romeo* is postponed for a year. Maybe it's all for the best, by the time it emerges it ought to be deeply seasoned, cured, hung, aged in the wood."

This marked the second halt for the project. The first had occurred when Bernstein and Laurents had become involved in the musicalization of James M. Cain's *Serenade*, not long before Warner Brothers announced that they would film the Cain story with Mario Lanza as the leading man. In 1955, Bernstein went to Hollywood to do the score for Elia Kazan's *On the Waterfront*, and he ran into Laurents the afternoon of August 25, at the Beverly Hills Hotel pool. Laurents was doing the screenplay for *Summertime*, a movie based on his own play, *The Time of the Cuckoo*. The two men reminisced and lamented the fact that their earlier idea of a modern-day Romeo and Juliet story had not worked out. They recall in *Sondheim & Co.* that while talking, they noticed a *Los Angeles Times* headline about gang fights between Mexicans and so-called Americans: "Gang Riots on Oliveira Street." "Arthur and I looked at one another and all I can say is that there are moments which are right for certain things and that moment seemed to have come." Bernstein suggested: "What about doing it about the Chicanos?" In New York there were Puerto Rican gangs, and at the time papers were filled with stories about juvenile delinquents and their violent crimes. "Suddenly it all springs to life," Bernstein recorded in his diary for that day. "I hear rhythms and pulses, and — most of all — I can sort of feel the form."

Upon their return to New York, they contacted Jerome Robbins, who became wildly excited at the prospect of a feasible Romeo story. Bernstein madly agreed to take on the lyrics as well as the music, but the latter turned out to be (as he says in Peyser's biography) "extraordinarily balletic, and there was tremendously more music — symphonic and balletic than anything I had anticipated. I realized then I couldn't do all the lyrics and do them well." A call was made to Betty Comden and Adolph Green, who worked out a six-page typewritten story plan (entitled *Romeo*) that contained a lot of jukebox jitterbug and that ended with a swooning Juliet in a reprise of the balcony scene. Except for the Puerto Ricans, the gang members had names from Shakespeare's tragedy, and the first balcony scene moved from dialogue to song to dialogue. However, Comden and

Green were committed to a Hollywood movie, so Robbins, Bernstein, and Laurents searched for an alternative.

Laurents mentioned that he had heard a young fellow named Stephen Sondheim sing some of his songs at an audition for the *Serenade* project. Actually, Sondheim had sung from *Saturday Night*, his first professional job in the musical theatre, which never came to fruition after its chief producer, Lemuel Ayers, suddenly died. Stephen Sondheim's Broadway career appeared to have halted before it ever began. But George Oppenheimer raved about Sondheim to Martin Gabel who arranged the audition. Then the *Serenade* project also died. However, Sondheim's effort was rewarded when, at the invitation of Burt Shevelove, he attended an opening-night party for *Isle of Goats* at the apartment of Ruth Ford and Zachary Scott. Sondheim is quoted by Craig Zadan as saying that he did not know anyone there, except for Shevelove. He did spot Arthur Laurents in a corner, and went over to make small talk. He discovered that Laurents was just about to begin a musical of *Romeo and Juliet* with Bernstein and Robbins. "Who's doing the lyrics?" he asked. Laurents suddenly remembered Sondheim's audition and "smote his forehead": "I never thought of you and I liked your lyrics a lot." He invited the young composer "to meet and play for Bernstein."

Sondheim told Bernstein that he did not want to write *just* lyrics. Then he played him the score of *Saturday Night*. "I went wild," remarked Bernstein. "I thought that he was a real, honest-to-God talent. The music wasn't terribly distinguished — it sounded like anybody's music — but the lyrics didn't sound like anybody's lyrics by any means."

Sondheim was absolutely sincere about not wanting to write lyrics to someone else's music. He told his mentor Oscar Hammerstein that he wouldn't accept the job if it were offered to him, but Hammerstein coaxed him into accepting the opportunity to work with first-rate professionals on a project that sounded exciting.

"It was a difficult decision for Steve to make," comments Milton Babbitt, one of Sondheim's *avant-garde* teachers in New York. "Steve had always regarded himself as primarily a composer and for a long time he felt humiliated a little bit — certainly put upon — and certainly a bit embarrassed that he was to be regarded as a man of words, a lyric writer."

Sondheim's agent, Flora Roberts, recalls in *Sondheim & Co.* that Sondheim rehearsed every conceivable excuse not to accept the job: "Steve would complain, 'I can't do this show. . . . I've never been that poor and I've never *known* a Puerto Rican.'"

★ ★ ★

Born on March 22, 1930, Sondheim was the son of a successful New York dress manufacturer. He was a child prodigy who read the *New York Times* in the first grade. His musical training was sporadic — Craig Zadan reports: "He had a year of piano when he was seven, a year of organ at eleven, a year of piano at fourteen, and another year at nineteen" — but he happened to be in the right place at the right time. After her marriage fell apart, his mother moved to a farm in Pennsylvania, where Sondheim befriended Jimmy Hammerstein, whose father was the renowned musical composer, Oscar, who happened to be working on *Oklahoma!* at the time. Oscar Hammerstein became a surrogate father to the boy, and when he noticed young Sondheim's musical talent, he quickly took him under his wing, offering incisive lessons in musicianship and composition. At first, these lessons took a heavy toll on the boy's ego. When, at fifteen, Sondheim rushed to Hammerstein with a musical he had composed about campus life, Hammerstein called the work "the worst thing I've ever read." Then seeing the lad's lower lip beginning to tremble, he added: "Now, I didn't say that it was untalented, I said it was terrible. And if you want to know *why* it's terrible, I'll tell you." As Hammerstein cut his way from the very first stage direction through every song and line of dialogue, Sondheim realized that he was receiving "the distillation of thirty years of experience." Hammerstein was actually honouring him by treating him as a fellow professional and not simply as a bright and naively eager adolescent. Hammerstein taught him to structure a song like a one-act play and to say what he truly wanted to say. He taught him the value and utter necessity of simplicity, how to introduce character, make songs relate to character, how to tell a story, and the interrelationship between lyric and music. Then Hammerstein outlined a six-year course of study, and asked Sondheim to write four distinctive types of musicals. Sondheim explained to Zadan: the first was to be an adaptation of "a play that I admired"; the second was to be an adaptation of "a play I didn't think was very good"; the third was to be a musical treatment of a novel or a short story; and the fourth was to be a true original. Sondheim duly complied with his mentor's suggestions. He first adapted *Beggar on Horseback* by George S. Kaufman and Marc Connelly, and actually received permission to do it for three performances at college. Next, he adapted Maxwell Anderson's *High Tor*, which taught him something about structure and editing and focus. However, Anderson wanted to collaborate with Kurt Weill on a musical from the play, and so Sondheim was not granted performance rights. For his third effort, "I spent about a year writing a musical version of *Mary Poppins*. That's where I encountered the real difficulties of playwriting." His climactic project, completed when he finished college, was called *Climb High* and was bulky rather than elevated: its ninety-nine-page first act alone was as long as Rodgers and Hammerstein's *South Pacific*. When Hammerstein read the script, he circled page 99 and added a single word: "Wow!"

On graduating from Williams College, Sondheim received the Hutchinson Prize, a two-year fellowship that he used to study under Milton Babbitt, professor of music at Princeton and the leading advocate of serialism. Although erudite to a fault in his approach to music, Babbitt loved American popular music, and he spent the first half-hour of each lesson with Sondheim analyzing Kern, Berlin, da Sylva, Brown, and Henderson, before turning to the "serious" music of Mozart sonatas and Beethoven symphonies. Babbitt discovered that his young student had "a very nimble mind" and was "very musical," though Sondheim "worked slowly, even on what might seem to be simple material." Part of the reason for this slow pace was his sense of perfection — he took "a long time to satisfy himself" — and part was his great fondness for parties and intricate games or puzzles.

Sondheim's colleagues would later become prominent in show business. One of these was Harold Prince, whom he first met at the opening night of *South Pacific* in 1948; another was Burt Shevelove, who later collaborated with Larry Gelbart in writing *A Funny Thing Happened on the Way to the Forum*. Babbitt recalls that when things were difficult, Shevelove and Sondheim would call each other up to see who had finished the London *Times* crossword puzzle first. Other than writing birthday songs for friends, Sondheim never wrote a song without a dramatic situation as a basis. Shevelove remembers in *Sondheim & Co.* that his friend always thought "in terms of theater music. He never said, 'I have a melody here' or 'Wouldn't this be a cute idea for a song?' He still can't think in those terms. He's the only nonopera writer of true theater music around today."

Sondheim had much to learn from Shevelove, who stressed clarity of language and thought. In *They're Playing Our Song*, Sondheim explains to Max Wilk: "Burt advised me, 'Never sacrifice smoothness for cleverness. Better dull than clumsy.' I agree. An awful lot of lyrics suffer from the lyric-writer having a really clever, sharp idea which he can't quite fit into the music, so it sits there clumsily and the actor is stuck with singing it. The net result is that it doesn't land with the audience."

Sondheim's contact with figures from the entertainment world was widened by his friendship with Oscar Hammerstein. He was introduced to George Oppenheimer, then a television producer, who, in turn, put him in touch with Martin Gabel, the producer of the ill-fated *Serenade*. Several months after an audition for Gabel came the opening-night party when Sondheim met Laurents. The ball for *West Side Story* began to roll seriously.

The question of style cropped up again once Sondheim was part of the team. All four collaborators knew what they did not want, and Laurents would later articulate this in the *New York Herald Tribune*: "Neither formal poetry nor flat reportage; neither opera nor split-level musical comedy numbers; neither zippered-in ballets nor characterless dance routines. We didn't want newsreel acting, blue-jean costumes or garbage-can scenery any more than we wanted soapbox pounding for our theme of young love destroyed by a violent world of prejudice." About a year earlier, when *Candide* had prevented his working on this project, Bernstein had noted in his diary that the *Romeo* musical was "a problematical work" that needed the benefit of "as much sitting time" as it could get. "Chief problem: to tread the fine line between opera and Broadway, between realism and poetry, ballet and 'just dancing,' abstract and representational. Avoid being 'messagy.' "

Bernstein would receive sole credit for the score, but Sondheim would share the credit for the lyrics. Joan Peyser explains the business angle: "Because music and lyrics together were to receive four percent of the royalties, Bernstein would get three percent for doing the music and half of the lyrics and Sondheim one percent for his half of the lyrics."

After the *Candide* fiasco, Bernstein was determined not to allow anything to come between him and the *Romeo* project. He wrote in his diary: "From here on nothing shall disturb the project; whatever happens to interfere I shall cancel summarily. It's going too well now to let it drop again."

Yet, the project was bedevilled once again. The big issue was the matter of a producer. George Abbott, who was directing *New Girl in Town*, turned it down. Richard Rodgers, who had long known Sondheim and whose daughter Mary was a friend of the young lyricist, also turned it down. As did Oscar Hammerstein and Leland Hayward. Harold Prince, Sondheim's pal from the Williams College days, also rejected it initially, even before hearing the score. One of his reasons was his involvement as coproducer with Robert E. Griffith in *New Girl in Town*, starring Gwen Verdon. A second reason was his failure to recognize just how artfully concise Laurents' book was. The general opinion of the nay-sayers was that it was an angry, unpleasant show, with too much violence and street language, and two dead bodies on stage at the end of the first act. Roger Stevens was the only one who wanted to gamble on the show, but he did not want to do it solo. So, a backers' audition was held, at which Bernstein, Laurents, Robbins, and Sondheim did their best presentations on behalf of the project. Bernstein recalled: "We all got up and did our damndest. It was an apartment on the East River. There was no air-conditioning. The windows were open and there were a lot of tugboats. Later we put the tugboat sound into the score."

The audition failed to raise a single cent. "No one should be shocked by that," comments Robbins in *Broadway Song & Story*. "A *fait accompli* is one thing, but it's not surprising that people said, 'I don't understand what that's about' in the case of a work in the embryo stage that was quite radical in its time. They hadn't heard Lenny's score, they hadn't read the script, they certainly hadn't seen what was going to be danced."

Cheryl Crawford did say yes, and she had sterling credentials, with a history of involvement with major dramatic enterprises. A midwesterner by birth, she was first associated with the Provincetown Players in the 1920s and the Theatre Guild in its heyday. Then, with Lee Strasberg and Harold Clurman, she had founded and run the prestigious Group Theatre, an ancestor of the Actors Studio, which she later cofounded with Elia Kazan and Robert Lewis. She had also helped ANTA (American National Theatre Academy) come into being as a non-profit body, and she dedicated herself to taking the best available theatre to every state in the union. Along with Eva Le Gallienne and Margaret Webster, she cofounded the American Repertory Company, and independently produced such famous shows as *Porgy and Bess* (1942), *One Touch of Venus* (1943), *Galileo* (1947) with Charles Laughton, *Brigadoon* (1947), *Paint Your Wagon* (1951), *The Rose Tattoo* (1951) with Maureen Stapleton, *Camino Real* (1953) with Eli Wallach, *Sweet Bird of Youth* (1959) with Geraldine Page, *Andorra* (1963), and *Mother Courage* (1963).

Things looked fine at first, but then something went strangely wrong. She reportedly played one artistic collaborator against another, spreading hurtful gossip and undermining everyone's contribution. Laurents delivered a devastating account of her behaviour in *Sondheim & Co.*: "Cheryl was known as a lady of great morality, but not the way she behaved on this show. For one thing she would say to me, 'You can't listen to Jerry, he doesn't know anything about writing.' And she would go to Jerry and say, 'You've got to do something about Arthur!'" She wanted the show to explain why the poor in New York were now predominantly Puerto Rican or black and not Jewish any longer. At one point she even questioned Laurents' special slang, wondering why no character ever said, "That's how the cookie crumbles." On the one hand, she claimed to be wanting a more realistic treatment of the story — with an explanation of why the youth were the way they were — and not a poetic interpretation. But, on the other hand, Bernstein claims in *Broadway Song & Story* that she commented, "We have *had* this whole school of ash can realism."

In her autobiography, *One Naked Individual*, she presents her version of why she went cold on the show. Her main concern, she claims, was the exorbitant cost for producing the show — a cost which would exceed that of any other show she had produced. She worried about the lack of financial backers. Then, she was discouraged by Rodgers and Hammerstein's feeling that it would be difficult to find youngsters who could sing Bernstein's score. "In this mood, I restudied the book," she claims. "It was thin, somehow . . . and really, there wasn't any leavening, any humor . . . (The one funny song was added later)."

Six weeks before rehearsals were due to begin, she met with the collaborators in her office. Her tone was more angry than agonized, and she insisted that the libretto explain why the gang members were the way they were. She rejected contentions that the play was a poetic fantasy rather than a sociological document. "You have to rewrite the whole thing or I won't do it," she declared adamantly. The four men rose simultaneously and silently, and walked out. Joan Peyser recounts that they first "went to the Algonquin Hotel but were not admitted because Laurents wasn't wearing a tie. Then they walked to the Iroquois Hotel, where Laurents used a public telephone and called [Roger] Stevens collect in London." Laurents reported to his three colleagues: "Roger says, whatever happens, keep working. He will guarantee everything somehow. Just don't worry about it." This was what Bernstein called "the life saver," for in that single moment Stevens "gave us the strength to have the courage of our own somewhat shaken convictions."

That same night, Sondheim telephoned Hal Prince and Robert Griffith in Boston, where they were trying out *New Girl in Town*, a musical version of *Anna Christie*. Prince and Griffith lamented that Verdon was ill and out of their show and that rehearsals were stymied. After a mutual exchange of sympathies, Sondheim said: "We don't have a producer." "Why don't you send the material to Bobby and me?" suggested Prince. Sondheim was flabbergasted, because a few years earlier Prince had said *West Side Story* wasn't for him. Prince had still not seen the script, but he and Griffith agreed to fly into New York to hear the score. He warned that he and his partner would have to return promptly to Boston, where Abbott was desperately trying to cure an ailing show. In essence, Prince was negotiating for time and priorities: yes, he and his partner would commit whole-heartedly to *West Side Story*, but only after *New Girl in Town* was put properly on her feet.

When Prince and Griffith arrived in New York, Sondheim and Bernstein played the score, and soon Prince was singing along with them. As Prince recollected in his memoirs, Bernstein was amazed: "My God, he's so musical! A *musical* producer!" Then, putting *West Side Story* out of their minds, Prince and Griffith returned to Boston. *New Girl* opened on Broadway on May 14, 1957; the two met with Robbins, Bernstein, Laurents, and Sondheim at 10 a.m. the next morning. Prince declared candidly: "First, that opening song 'Mix' is out. It hits the wrong note to begin with." Sondheim, Laurents, Bernstein, and Robbins nodded, relieved that someone else had decided what they had postponed for months. A deal was on — and so was *Gangway!* (as the show was called at the time). It took only a week to raise the $350,000 budgeted for the production.

★   ★   ★

Prince is regarded as one of the most controversial creative forces on the Broadway scene today, and even when he started as producer (along with Robert Griffith), he surprised many experienced colleagues by his bold enterprises and relentless commitment to shows that often looked unprepossessing artistically or commercially. His career up to 1957 was marked by some missteps — as any producer's or director's would be — but was remarkable for its ambition, training, and risks.

Harold Smith Prince was born on January 30, 1928, to privileged Jewish parents of German stock whose families had settled in New York City soon after the Civil War. He was raised by his kind stepfather (because his own father, who lived to a ripe old age, rarely saw him). This stepfather was a Wall Street stockbroker, who possibly passed on his business acumen to him. Prince's mother, who was an avid theatregoer, probably fostered his enthusiasm for the stage. "Saturday matinées were part of a New York Jewish child's intellectual upbringing," he claimed in *Contradictions*, and "I spent mine in the orchestra with my parents, or in the top balcony with a schoolfriend or by myself. My allowance went for theatre tickets rather than for ball games, and I saw Orson Welles when he was twenty-one do *Julius Caesar*, Burgess Meredith in *Winterset*, [Tallulah] Bankhead in *The Little Foxes*, and [Joseph] Schildkraut and [Eva] Le Gallienne together in *Uncle Harry*. . . . I wasn't as interested in musicals, and by the time I got to the University of Pennsylvania [at age sixteen], I wasn't interested in them at all."

In his memoirs he describes his experiences in college and after: he formed a university radio station and wrote weekly adaptations of plays, pirating everything from O'Neill, Maxwell Anderson, and Odets. He would direct these and occasionally act in them as well. He was not a drama major — simply because there was no such thing at the time, and he didn't believe that college programs could provide valuable, practical experience. He finished his liberal-arts education at nineteen, and managed to work for George Abbott a year later, avoiding summer stock because he did not believe in the apprenticeship system.

He was bold but lucky. Lazy about actively looking for work, he wrote plays which he thought would "make the rounds." "One of these reached the head of the script department at ABC-TV," who sent Prince for an interview to the George Abbott office where Abbott was planning a "small experimental TV unit." Prince "offered to work 'on spec' for nothing" and was accepted. Two weeks later, however, he was put on the payroll at $25 a week, remaining at that salary for six months. He did a little of everything for the three television shows the company produced. One was a modest musical called *The Hugh Martin Show*, written by Abbott and featuring Hugh Martin, Joan McCracken, the Hugh Martin Singers, Butterfly McQueen (of *Gone with the Wind* fame), and comedienne Kaye Ballard. But Prince clashed with Ballard, and Martin delivered an ultimatum to Abbott: choose between Prince and the show. Abbott chose Prince, and the Sunday-night show went off the air.

Abbott proved to be a good-luck charm, because even after he disbanded the whole television operation — the projects weren't making money, and there was too much hysteria in the office — Abbott recommended Prince as a replacement for Robert Griffith's unsatisfactory stage manager on a revue called *Touch and Go* written by Jean and Walter Kerr. Prince's salary was $75 a week, and he ran the switchboard, helped with casting, and delivered messages as the show, which had originated at Catholic University in Washington, D.C., made its frothy way to the Broadhurst in October, 1949, where it died after 176 performances.

For Prince, things began to move quickly. At night, he was assistant stage manager at the Broadhurst; by day, he did general jobs in the Abbott office. But a show in Boston called *Tickets, Please* was in trouble. Abbott, who had taken over after its original director was fired, needed a stage manager. Griffith was in London, staging a version of *Touch and Go*, so Prince went to Boston in his stead. *Tickets, Please*, starring Paul and Grace Hartman, opened on April 27, 1950, and ran a season. By the end of the run, Prince had written a comedy-murder mystery, called *A Perfect Scream*, in collaboration with Ted Luce. The Hartmans optioned the play and Prince promptly joined the Dramatists Guild. However, the Hartman marriage fell apart and with this, any chance of a production of the play.

Prince did not have much time to be upset. He was loaned by Abbott to the Leland Hayward office to cast the Irving Berlin musical, *Call Me Madam*. It was also understood that he would be Griffith's first assistant on the show. He made important contacts with people who would play significant roles in his future. One was Ruth Mitchell, Hayward's stage manager on *Mister Roberts*. Other contacts were Howard Lindsay and Russel Crouse, who later became devoted supporters and investors. But he never got to work on *Madam* because the Korean War started and he was among the first draftees. He spent two years in Germany, assigned to an anti-aircraft artillery battalion, but he never forgot Abbott's promise that there would be a job awaiting him upon his return. His arrival home in October, 1952, coincided with the opening of Abbott's production of *In Any Language*, starring Uta Hagen and Walter Matthau, and he was given passes for the evening, so he made for the Cort Theatre, where he arrived fifteen minutes before the curtain to find Abbott and Griffith. In *Contradictions*, he recalls the conversation: "Are you back already?" Abbott asked. "It's been two years," Prince retorted. "When do you get out?" "Next week." "Well, come in next week. We're doing a show with Rosalind Russell based on *My Sister Eileen*."

This was *Wonderful Town*, which brought Prince into contact with Betty Comden and Adolph Green, as well as with Leonard Bernstein and Jerome Robbins. A significant network of artistic relationships was thus established, but even more important than this was the fact that Prince had an invaluable opportunity to learn how a successful musical was created, and his teacher was none other than the masterly George Abbott.

Wonderful Town opened on February 25, 1953, at the Winter Garden and ran over 500 performances. During the first year of its success, Prince and Griffith hatched plans for coproducing their own show. Born in Methuen, Massachusetts, in 1907, Griffith had begun his career as an actor. He had appeared in the original Broadway productions of *Once in a Lifetime*, *Dinner at Eight*, and *Merrily We Roll Along*. After he became Abbott's chief stage manager in 1935, he was associated with more than fifty productions, including *Three Men on a Horse*, *Best Foot Forward*, *Call Me Madam*, and *Where's Charley?*. He was a shy, easygoing man, over twenty years senior to Prince, and he was introverted. Prince, in contrast, was more dynamic and volatile. But their differences in age, background, and temperament were not barriers to a partnership, for both had been groomed by Abbott, and both were ambitious. Griffith was interested in musicalizing a book by Richard Bissell called *7½¢*, about a strike in a pajama factory. Abbott was not interested because the story seemed drab and too risky for a social climate where strikes, labour, and strike leaders were being pilloried by the McCarthy Committee. But out of affection for Griffith, Abbott agreed to direct if the adaptation was suitable. Prince and Griffith had no money — not even for stationery — so Abbott provided everything, including an office and telephones, without ever billing them. The two producers did their own secretarial work and raised their $250,000 budget for *The Pajama Game* by auditioning for backers in borrowed living rooms. Frederick Brisson, Rosalind Russell's husband, came on board, but the producers were only able to pay rent after their show opened on May 13, 1954, with an advance sale of $40,000, barely guaranteeing a week's run.

The Pajama Game became a stunning début for Prince and Griffith. It launched Bob Fosse as a hit choreographer, provided Jerome Robbins with his first directorial opportunity, established Richard Adler and Jerry Ross as a songwriting team, and made Carol Haney the sparkling "new face" on Broadway. Another landmark was the fact that the show became a hit in May, just before summer, a period which is not usually good for business. It ran for over 1,000 performances and won the Antoinette Perry and Donaldson Awards as the best musical of the season. Warner Brothers produced a movie version in 1957, starring Doris Day, hired most of the stage cast, and brought in Abbott to codirect with Stanley Donen.

Griffith and Prince became involved in their second project just a couple of weeks after *The Pajama Game* had begun its run. Abbott had agreed to direct a musical based on *The Year the Yankees Lost the Pennant*, a novel by Douglas Wallop. But his proviso was that Frederick Brisson, Griffith, and Prince produce it. This was no problem, and the show went into production with Adler and Ross responsible for the score, Fosse for the choreography, and Abbott and Wallop attempting the adaptation. Baseball did not easily lend itself to Broadway musical comedy, but despite the poor record of past baseball plays, the project moved ahead and became *Damn Yankees*, with Gwen Verdon in the leading role, which had been turned down by Mitzi Gaynor and ZiZi Jeanmaire. A great deal of material was rewritten on the road. As Prince recalled: "More than one-third of the score was jettisoned. All the ingredients for panic were there but

Abbott worked calmly, and day by day everything improved except the ending." When the show opened on Broadway on May 5, 1955, Verdon, who had been playing a beautiful witch, turned into an ugly hag at the curtain. The audience resented this because it had fallen in love with Verdon's Lola. The day after the opening, Griffith, Prince, Abbott, and the songwriters called a rehearsal for cuts and readjustments, and Verdon was changed back into a beautiful seductress. *Damn Yankees* played 1,012 performances and won the Tony for best musical.

The Pajama Game and *Damn Yankees* revealed significant patterns in the Griffith-Prince partnership. First, there was a deliberate attraction to apparently unprepossessing and unconventional material. Second, there was a willingness to base business judgements on artistic criteria. Third, there was little advance publicity for the shows, which increased the opportunity for surprises. Fourth, there was a gamble on non-stars in central roles. Carol Haney was a newcomer — as was her understudy, Shirley Maclaine, who went on in her place one night and was discovered by movie producer Hal Wallis. Gwen Verdon, who had been acclaimed in 1953 for her dancing in *Can-Can*, was not considered a star until *Damn Yankees*. The Griffith-Prince predilection for non-stars was rooted in the belief that (in Prince's words) "It is not unusual for material to get short shrift, for otherwise good material to seem inferior, in the hands of a dazzling personality. Stars have a way of saving themselves at the cost of the material." Prince did not object to casting a star if that person happened to be the best for a role, but he took satisfaction from the fact that the theatre didn't really permit the star system to work.

New Girl in Town was the end of the three-way partnership, for once Brisson moved back to California, Griffith and Prince consolidated their own production company and took over *West Side Story*. Griffith was thorough and patient, having absorbed much of George Abbott's level-headed knowledge of the practical side of theatre. Prince was also disciplined, but he liked to have a final say in almost every creative decision, not out of egotistic self-indulgence, but because of a need to preserve an artistic vision and to control a business enterprise. With their involvement in *West Side Story*, Prince and Griffith were both ready to reshape their careers without Abbott's direct assistance. Abbott counselled them against getting involved in the gang musical, which was far, indeed, from the sort of material Abbott liked to direct, but Prince trusted his own instincts and was relieved to finally get Abbott's blessing.

Designing Trio

EVEN AFTER THE OVERALL BUDGET was quickly raised, there was a delay in the production process because Jerome Robbins insisted that Oliver Smith redesign his sets. When Smith first brought in his designs, Robbins was critical. "Where's your close-in in one so we can work in one while you're changing the sets behind?" "Well, we're not going to do that," Smith countered. "Wait a minute! What's happening?" Robbins wondered to himself. Many of the sets were sectional, and the director wondered how to choreograph clean entrances and exits, and how to light the sets.

He needn't have worried unduly, because his design team was extraordinarily gifted, experienced, and harmonious. Robbins had a trio that was the envy of many another director.

Oliver Smith had fled to New York from Penn State when a wealthy relative promised him a course at the Yale Drama School, provided Smith could make his own living for a year. Arriving in New York with $80, he proceeded to hold his life together with an assortment of jobs, working as a Roxy usher, a stock clerk at Stern's, and a bookstamper in the Flatbush library. Fascinated by the city, and considering himself to be comfortably off with $20 a week, he decided to forego Yale. In 1942, at the ripe age of twenty-four, he launched his career as scenic designer with the Ballets Russes de Monte Carlo for Massine's *Saratoga*. This led to *Rodeo*, Agnes de Mille's landmark ballet. Two years later he did his first work for American Ballet Theatre, designing sets for *Fancy Free*, the Robbins-Bernstein ballet that later became *On the Town*. After a few more shows, he was asked by Lucia Chase to become codirector. "We were only going to do it for a couple of years," Smith reminisced, "but we ended up working together for thirty-five." Ballet design was of

50

great importance to his artistic development and maturity. As he remarked to Audrey Farolino: "I believe very much that ballet design is of very great importance for anyone who wants to work in the theater, because you have to learn economy of space, you have to understand fantasy, and have a poetic sense that brings that all out."

Tall, courtly Smith did not confine himself to the rarefied atmosphere of ballet; he branched out into Broadway, creating décor for *Rosalinda* (1942), *Billion Dollar Baby* (1945), *Brigadoon* (1947), *High Button Shoes* (1947), *Gentlemen Prefer Blondes* (1949), *Paint Your Wagon* (1951), *La Traviata* at the Met, and a revival of *Pal Joey* (1952) that challenged the received vocabularies and ideas of critics. His method of preparing for musicals was different from that for straight plays, in that for a musical he read the book only "once and never again" (as he revealed in a 1970 *Plays and Players* interview) because it was usually very poor. For straight plays, he read more carefully before attempting to empty his mind of everything else. "I get into a blank state and do a great deal of thinking," he explained. "Once I start, I work very rapidly, often on an architectural floor plan; while I'm drawing the master plan I visualise the details so when I've finished I know exactly how it's going to look. Then I make sketches of the elevations."

My Fair Lady (1956) was an exception to this rule, for Smith began with a sketch of the study, Higgins' imperial domain and a palpable Edwardian emblem, before proceeding with other settings that combined the sculptural, the architectural, and the painterly to masterly effect. Stylish, without being overly fussy, his décor for that show ranged from the crazy squalor of Covent Garden and the gaslit living rooms to the dazzling pavilions of Ascot and the icy grandeur of an embassy ballroom.

His challenge with *West Side Story* was to make an essentially urban world into both a jungle of brick, concrete, and steel and a microcosmic paradise of romantic neon and gaudy streamers. For the most part, Smith spent his days at his house on Long Island, only forty miles from the seaside home of Arthur Laurents, with whom he discussed sets. For the first time in his life, he began designing with models and not sketches. Having created many New York backgrounds with sensational skylines, he conceived of *West Side Story* (or *Gangway!* as his working sketches were titled) in terms of the Renaissance. He wanted to give the show a broad sweep of colour. He would open it out beyond the limitations of the narrow streets, alleys, playgrounds, rotting plaster-and-brick walls, and mesh-wire fences. Initially, Laurents disliked his ideas, but Smith drew Jerome Robbins' empathy. So, scores of quiet pencil sketches appeared under his name — of doorways, sectional walls, free-floating fire escapes, massive arches, girders, drugstore, and small bedroom — and then colour washes with specific details of texture and geometry. His Romeo and Juliet would play their balcony scene on a fire escape, and their first meeting at a gym dance would be fringed with light metal arches and decorated with multicoloured streamers. For the Sharks-Jets rumble, he would have colour washes for a brooding sky. His designs used urban textures — wood, brick, stone, concrete, plaster, steel — in ways that had a sinister formality without sacrificing the insistent romantic counterpoint. The floating fire escapes suggested a breathless isolation, the shabby tenement walls of a bedroom whirled away, fences and windows disappeared in the doomed lovers' defiant freedom. And the blend of concrete and abstract décors, the authentic vibrancy and chaos of alleys and tenements, imparted a visual excitement.

The show's costume designer was Irene Sharaff, a long-legged woman with heavily mascaraed eyes, a sense of *haute couture*, and a list of credits that would already have been enough to light up Broadway. Born in Boston and educated at the New York School of Fine and Applied Arts and at Le Grand Chaumier in Paris, she had had an élite training. In the summer of 1928, she met Aline Bernstein, the scenic and costume designer who had just become the artistic director of The Civic Repertory Theatre. Bernstein enlisted her to draft blueprints for scenery, prepare costume and prop lists, and help with other chores. Four years later, Sharaff designed *Alice in Wonderland*, using white sailcloth as a basic fabric for both scenery and costumes, drawing on it with brushstrokes that were, she explained in her memoir, "similar in form and application to the fine cross-hatched pen lines of Tenniel's technique (though proportionately broader, of course, to carry the effect across the footlights)." Background and scenery were "drawn on a huge scroll like a typewriter ribbon, fed scene by scene from a spool on the left across the back of the stage to a spool on the right. Small pieces of constructed scenery needed in some scenes moved on two small flat wagons on sunken tracks across the stage. All scene changes took place in full view of the audience." The entire production was designed in black and white, except for Alice's blue dress, an oversized red Victorian chair, and the Red Queen's crimson robe. This design won Sharaff her first Donaldson Award, and was merely the beginning of a legendary career. Her sense of innovation was exemplary. For Moss Hart's revue, *As Thousands Cheer* (1933), she designed the Easter Parade section, taking her cue from the rotogravure section of the *New York Times* Sunday edition. Setting the period back to 1885, she designed costumes in a wide range of browns from the lightest to the darkest, and from warm tones to cold, "strategically using touches of cool and warm whites among the bitter chocolate brown, umbers, siennas, and taupes." The colours and fabrics reproduced a glossy sepia effect in theatrical terms.

Her first opportunity to design costumes for an entire Broadway musical came with *On Your Toes* (1936). For the "Scheherazade" take-off, she gave the late-18th-century look strong Persian accents, crossing cultures and styles with free fantasy, giving the male dancers "Persian jackets with the inevitable tights," and the females, short tutus, transparent pantaloons, bodices cut like Persian jackets, and large white hats, like (she explained) "immense poufs of whipped cream, such as the Incroyables in France affected at that time." In the other ballet, "Slaughter on Tenth Avenue," the palette had shades of sienna, dusty pink, indigo, and violet, but the two principals, Ray Bolger and Tamara Geva, wore black and white in sharp contrast.

Sharaff had an extraordinary number of successes for producers as diverse as Eva Le Gallienne and Mike Todd, Jr., and for scripts that ran the gamut from Robert Sherwood and Shakespeare to Clifford Odets and Betty Comden and Adolph Green. Her privileged background and experience (she had visited Paris in 1931, coming under the inspiring influences of *haute couture*, Cirques d'Hiver, and Alexandre Benois) gave her a distinct edge over other designers who had known nothing like her exposure to the work of Christian Bérard, Pavel Tchelitchev, and André Derain in Parisian theatre. Her career mounted quickly, with particular successes in *The Boys from Syracuse* (1938), *By Jupiter* (1942), *Billion Dollar Baby* (1945), and *Candide* (1956).

Perhaps her most stunning costume design came in three different productions of *The King and I* — the original 1951 Broadway version, the 1953 London edition, and the 1956 film. The intersection of Western and Oriental cultures in a Siamese setting fired her imagination, and she spent her budget on Thai silks, Chinese damasks and brocades, silkscreened cottons, and other fabrics woven in India, Japan, and Hong Kong. Every costume was a work of art, but none more so than Yul Brynner's *panung* (loin cloth gathered up into a sophisticated knickerbocker) or Gertrude Lawrence's dusty pink satin ball gown, whose puffed sleeves looked in Sharaff's words, "like two small wings" and whose snood, like a net made of silk cord with shimmering paillettes, imparted the sense of a gracious guardian angel with an independent mind.

Sharaff's work for film was no less distinguished. Her first musical film had been *Meet Me in St. Louis* (1944), given a 1905 look, in which Mary Astor's dress in the finalé was executed in "strong net in fairly large mesh with small silk leaves sewn over it, and then appliquéd with tiny satin buttons and thin silk tendrils." Sharaff won her first Oscar for *An American in Paris* (1951), which evoked French Impressionist and post-Impressionist paintings while telling its story of the love between a young French girl (Leslie Caron) and an American painter (Gene Kelly). Her costume design captured perfectly the sense of various Parisian *quartiers*, and the six distinct sequences of the film rendered in the manner of six artists (Dufy, Renoir, Rousseau, Van Gogh, Utrillo, and Toulouse-Lautrec) required 300 costumes all fashioned according to the six styles.

But in one sense, all these past triumphs made her *West Side Story* assignment difficult, because this show had no place for exaggeration or fantasy, and yet literalness would not help visually. She went up to 110th Street to take notes on gang clothes. She also spent many "quiet and glorious moments" with Robbins as they discussed the characters. Her first sketches were in black and white, but then she conferred with Oliver Smith about colour. The show posed the familiar problem of demarcating two antithetical groups. Shakespeare had set a classic problem for designers with his Montagues and Capulets (for it was difficult to tell one from the other except by some costume code), but the modern, urban setting for *West Side Story* compounded the problem. Sharaff decided to rely on colour to contrast the two gangs, with touches of the Renaissance in the clothes. "In the fifties, the teen-age boys one saw on the streets of New York had arrived at a uniform of their own — not yet taken up as fashionable by men and women — consisting of blue jeans or chinos, T-shirts, windbreakers, and sneakers. . . . The modern windbreaker with a hood, particularly when worn with tight-fitting jeans, has a silhouette and line resembling that of figures in Florentine Renaissance paintings." The gangs wore windbreakers that "varied by using one colour in front, another in the back, with a sharp contrast in the colour of the sleeves." Sharaff explained: "The seams of the jackets were bound with narrow satin edging, again in contrasting color, so that as the dancers moved, their jackets seemed faceted in color. The T-shirt, which up to the fifties was worn solely as underwear, when dyed, gave the dancers the air of trapezists."

The Jets were in "muted indigo blues, ochre and musty yellows." The Sharks wore "sharp purple, pink-violet, blood red, and black." The colours were ingenious choices, seeming to suit the gang-members' physical appearances. Even though the Puerto Ricans were on the defensive, their outfits gave them an aggressive quality, and their girls, less uniform and more exotic, had brilliant colours, in startling contrast to the Jets' girls who wore pastels and seemed homogeneous. The only article of ethnic character worn by the Puerto Rican girls was the rebozo, a long woollen stole with fringed ends, worn around the shoulders and sometimes also over the head in Mexico and the Caribbean. As Sharaff recognized, "In the last scene, when the hero was shot, the rebozos over the girls' heads made them look like traditional figures of mourning."

Sharaff's design looked deceptively simple, and yet when Hal Prince sought to save money by substituting blue jeans from Levi Strauss in place of her trousers (when these became worn out), the look and effect were not the same. The substitutions looked like flat contemporary wear; Prince realized too late that they lacked the subtle character that Sharaff had imparted by use "of a special fabric, which was then dipped and dyed and beaten and dyed again and aged again." Her stage jeans "were in forty subtly different shades of blue, vibrating, energetic, creating the *effect* of realism."

Of course, neither Sharaff's costumes nor Oliver Smith's décor would have looked effective without Jean Rosenthal's lighting. A native New Yorker, she had begun her theatrical work at the Neighborhood Playhouse, attending to stage details for Martha Graham. She also worked at summer theatres, the Federal Theater project in New York, and managed the technical side of productions for the Municipal Wagon Theatre that played parks. She observed closely as the techniques of American stage lighting emerged during the Depression, when there was no money, no room, and little scenery. Next she studied lighting in classes given by Stanley McCandless at Yale, before moving on to the Parsons School of Design. She embarked on a professional career in 1935, serving as stage manager, production supervisor, and errand girl for the W.P.A. theatre project. A year later, when the man assigned to install lighting equipment for Leslie Howard's *Hamlet* fell ill, she was pressed into his job. Howard requested her services for the New York run and the road company, and she found that travelling with him was like travelling with royalty, for he received red carpet treatment throughout the country. The next year she became an all-round backstage participant in the Mercury Theatre, run by Orson Welles. For the opening production of a modern-dress *Julius Caesar*, she built platforms, shifted scenery, gave cues during performances, and lit the show. This production marked the first of several happy accidents in her career. During dress rehearsal, someone forgot to turn out the bald overhead working lights and when a blackout was called for, just before the Orchard Scene, these lights continued to shine through the grid from which ropes and pulleys were suspended. Winthrop Sargeant describes how

"A bewitching crisscross pattern of light was cast on stage, and Miss Rosenthal liked it so much that she incorporated it into the scene" to create "an impression of leafiness."

During World War II she interrupted her Broadway work to "compile a handbook on the electrical systems of cargo ships" (according to Sargeant's *New Yorker* profile), and she founded Theater Production Service, Inc. in 1940, manufacturing kits containing make-up, costumes, and portable scenic effects for G.I. theatricals overseas. In 1946, she took over lighting for the Ballet Society (which later became the New York City Ballet), designing for *The Medium* in 1947, and for several Martha Graham dances, believing that ballet, being purely visual, offered more leeway for imaginative lighting than did the theatre. In 1950, when the lighting cues for all productions in the New York City Opera's repertoire somehow got mislaid, she was called in to rescue the situation and in only six weeks she restored the lighting plans of fourteen operas.

The second of her great happy accidents occurred during the City Opera's production of *The Trial* by Gottfried von Einem (based on Kafka's novel). When a pulpit that was supposed to rise out of the floor got stuck halfway, the singer in the preacher's role appeared spectral as a result. The bisected preacher was regarded as a triumph of her surrealist imagination.

Perhaps her most stunning lighting effect, in Sargeant's opinion, was the one at the end of Graham's *The Cave*, when "the principal dancer's world suddenly turned to ash." Rosenthal devised "a wall of hot red light to be thrown against a backdrop" and to be intensified until the curtain fell. During the technical rehearsal, she asked an electrician to "wash it out," meaning to cut off all light, but he threw the switch for red first, leaving on some white ones; because of the violence of the reds, an optical illusion was created of a peculiarly cold gray-green that suggested ash.

Where Oliver Smith painted décor, she painted with light, her tools being batteries of spotlights, kliegs, scoop lights, and border lights. She treated lighting as an art, possessing what one critic called a "poetical idea of voltage." Everything had colour and form, but lighting was used to display that colour and form. Lighting bound together the shifting elements of a play or ballet, and when used to its fullest potential, it extended and heightened the dramatic mood. As she remarked in a 1955 *Sunday Mirror Magazine* feature, "Light on a stage should point up the effect of the music, the words, the scenery, the art of the performers, or whatever is on the stage."

A tiny, blue-eyed, curly-haired, dynamic woman, she saw her work as a collaboration in which her role was an extremely subtle one: "Everyone else — the actors, the directors, the producers, the writers — is the star, and you must go around and between all of them to see that things go as they should. And when no one in the audience knows where the light on the stage comes from, and when no one notices anything on the stage except the actors, the sets, the costumes, and the words and the music — then you know that you have done your job as it should be done."

Directors had been known to postpone Broadway openings in order to avail themselves of her skills. Actors and actresses trusted her implicitly, knowing that she would make them look attractive. As Winthrop Sargeant wrote, she was credited with carrying in her head an encyclopedic knowledge of the dimensions and lighting problems of every important theatre in the United States and abroad. "Fellow-professionals talk admiringly, if somewhat cryptically, of her 'cyclorama blues' and 'color washes.' Instructors who teach her obscure craft in college drama schools have analyzed her methods in standard textbooks on the subject." Her only chief rivals were Peggy Clark, a former scenic designer who now worked exclusively on Broadway, and Abe Feder, who did lighting for hotels, department stores, and convention halls, in addition to stage lighting. But Rosenthal's genius was for *suggesting* light and shade when the stage actually contained no shadow at all. As celebrated for the stark, eerie mud-coloured lighting of *The Medium* as for her "light-all-around" or wash effect, she was, by her own description in the *New Yorker*, "a regular magpie" who would use any discovery that she happened upon. Her happy accidents were, indeed, good luck, but it was her special genius to exploit the situations and convert accident into technique.

Rosenthal was the first lighting designer with whom Harold

Prince had ever collaborated. Before *West Side Story*, Robert Griffith and the company electrician, George Gebhardt, had lit his shows. As Prince revealed in *Contradictions: Notes on Twenty-six Years in the Theatre*, lighting design was largely unappreciated and, so, remained naive and non-artistic: "It was a matter of lights up for the scene, and lights down for the song. Lights up again after the song, with George Abbott shouting from the orchestra, 'more light on those faces — this is a funny scene.' And when the laughs didn't come, still more light." With Rosenthal's expertise, Prince could be assured of a deftly lit show, in which all the graceless beauty, tense horror, and aggressive energy would be revealed without pretentiousness.

As was her custom, she studied sketches of the sets, then read the script, imagining each scene before ever putting pencil to paper for the lighting plot. She imagined each cue, setting up the way the lights would change from moment to moment — whether it was a suggestion of early evening in an open street or a mere half-hour later in an intimate space, whether it was a blackout and a quick flood of multi-coloured light or a nocturnal balcony scene which was suddenly to melt with stars glowing through the dark wash of sky. As usual, she did ninety percent of the technical work in her head, going to paintings for ideas of chiaroscuro and sunless shadow. Because the show was a movement musical, at once realistic and stylized, she had the flexibility to be naturalistic as well as surrealistic. The result was strongly dramatic — sinister yet tender, joyous yet dangerous, gloomy yet transcendent.

The show could not let squalor be romantic, and she could not go all out for spectacular effects when everything depended on a sense of synoptic balance. In the final analysis, as Kenneth Pearson put it, "She used light as one would use water, sprinkling it on one actor, drenching another with everything she could find. Her lighting had to provide the atmosphere: the time of day, the beauty of a city. She found her pattern in a million neon signs." There was a classical economy, a firm discipline to the pattern. When chaos came on stage in the narrative, its images were subtly controlled by the unequalled mistress of dimmer, spot, and klieg.

Laurents' Book

DESPITE BEING TOUTED as a show conceived, directed, and choreographed by Robbins, *West Side Story* would not have materialized without Arthur Laurents' libretto. After all, the book is of primary importance in a musical, no matter how it is composed — whether in stages, after the playwright's consultations with director, musical composer, and lyricist, or whether drafted rather skimpily and then slowly expanded during the production process itself. In the case of this show, Laurents worked from an outline, consulted frequently with Robbins, Bernstein, and Sondheim, stuck faithfully to his task, and never sought to make his text draw attention to itself. He was wise enough to know that Broadway was becoming more and more a director's theatre because people such as Jerome Robbins carefully selected what they did, interpreting plays in such a way as to turn them into their very own productions. Not that Laurents was really concerned about the playwright's ego in opposition to the director's; what really interested him was providing a work that addressed part of the human condition as he perceived it in his time and place.

Laurents had a respectable reputation. Born in the Bronx (July 14, 1918), reared in the Flatbush section of Brooklyn, he had majored in English at Cornell University, and moved on to television, Broadway, and films after experiences in night-club revues and radio plays. During his enlistment years in a paratroop unit at Fort Benning, Georgia, he had worked on military training films, while also writing scripts for radio programs designed to educate the public about the problems of returning servicemen. *Assignment Home* won a Variety Poll Radio Award as one of the outstanding shows of 1945. Another script, *About Face*, was included in *The Best One-Act Plays of 1945–46*. After doing research for *Assignment Home*, Laurents was inspired to write his searing psychological drama about a battle- scarred Jewish ex-soldier who faces anti-Semitism. *Home of the Brave* opened to mixed reviews at the Belasco Theatre on Broadway in December, 1945, and even though it closed after only sixty-nine performances, many critics acknowledged it to be a significant contribution to postwar American theatre. Alas, the film version directed by Carl Foreman, which followed in 1949, turned the role of the Jew into a black man because Jews "had been done" in such movies as *Gentleman's Agreement*. Laurents, who had already failed with a second Broadway play in 1947, was angry, but persevered in a Hollywood career. He did the screenplays for *Rope* (1948), *The Snake Pit* (1948), and *Anna Lucasta* (1949).

Broadway and Hollywood shared his attention. After failing on stage with *The Bird Cage* (1950), a melodrama about the backstage troubles of a ruthlessly tyrannical cabaret owner, Laurents came up with a charming winner in *The Time of the Cuckoo* (1952), a rueful comedy about a lonely American spinster (played by Shirley Booth) who finds brief romance with a married Italian shopkeeper during a summer holiday in Venice. This hit won a Tony for Booth and was later filmed by David Lean with Katharine Hepburn, although with a new title, *Summertime* (1955).

Another Broadway play came after the film script for Anatole Litvak's *Anastasia* (1956), starring Ingrid Bergman. *A Clearing in the Woods* (1957), with Kim Stanley as a neurotic woman who confronts her past selves (played by three different actresses), was ambitious but laboured. It had only a three-and-a-half-week run. Yet Laurents persisted as a playwright, for he disliked the crass commercialism of Hollywood and the studios' tendency to dehumanize the profession. In theatre, he felt in contact with people; in Hollywood studios he heard only a clock, a cash register, and the anxieties of producers who wanted a product as quickly and as cheaply as possible. So, although he was reluctant to play second-fiddle to Bernstein on the project, he eagerly accepted the opportunity to write the script for a contemporary Romeo and Juliet story. He knew full well that his libretto would be but one element — albeit a fundamental one — in an integrated work, but the task of writing a story in which language was not to be of predominant concern was a fascinating technical challenge.

The musical-dance prologue is the first indication that the book does not intend language to be the prime vehicle for the story. Dance, movement, and music are so thoroughly integrated within the narrative that they become effective mirrors of the characters' minds and hearts, as well as being supple agents of dramatic power. In this way they lead to the innermost beings of the characters, leaving the language of the play to seem transparent, concise, and simple (sometimes simplistic). The wordplay of *Romeo and Juliet*, as M.M. Mahood shows, unites Shakespeare's images in a rich design, sharpens the play's dramatic irony, becomes an outlet for tumultuous feelings, and clarifies the conflicts of incompatible truths in a final equipoise. In contrast, the language of Laurents' libretto allows music, dance, and movement to appropriate many of the poetic means of creating the sense of tragedy.

Romeo and Juliet is the starting point of Laurents' adaptation and there are numerous intersections of Shakespeare's play and Laurents' libretto in the matters of theme, character, and plot, but there are also crucial divergences, chiefly in the quality and scope of language and the colorations of amorous passion. Where Shakespeare's wordplay conforms to Petrarchan and anti-Petrarchan conventions ("love as malady, as worship, as war, as conquest," according to Mahood), Laurents' invented slang and realistic vernacular are an attempt to distribute language across a narrow sociological area in order to shift the dramatic focus from character to environment. Laurents' play obviously lacks the fair dignity of Verona, although only a very naive person would fail to notice Shakespeare's irony in his choice of words, for, after all, the Capulets and Montagues bear an ancient grudge against one another, and the very first scene in a public place is marked by a fight that erupts among the two sets of servants before Prince Escalus' timely intervention. The deep-rooted family feud — whose precise genesis and history nobody appears to remember — pervades all social ranks in the two ancient houses, and is extended by the bawdy punning and violently low humour. In Laurents' American version, the servants Samson and Gregory are replaced by A-rab and Baby John, and the surly gangs speak of zip guns, switchblades, and bottles, and have their own low humour — as in A-rab's derisive imitation of a Puerto Rican accent ("Thees ees for stinkbombin' my old man's store") — but the issues here are specific: racial composition and territorial rights. Who owns the street? That is the question, and there is as yet no suggestion — as there is in Shakespeare — of a "death-mark'd love." There are other notable contrasts. While the foreground antagonists in Shakespeare are young, the family feud is an old one, so the parents and elders are radically culpable for the brewing conflicts. In Laurents, the gang members are all young, and the older generation (represented by Officer Krupke, plainclothes Schrank, Doc, and Glad Hand) serves as a dramatic foil.

But Shakespeare and Laurents do converge more closely in Scene 2, where the clichéd slogan ("Womb to tomb!"), introduced by glowing, slightly wacky Riff and repeated several times in the play, emblazons the idea of death and recalls Friar Laurence's identical theme: "The earth that's nature's mother is her tomb; / What is her burying grave, that is her womb" (2.3.9–10). Tony, the vernacular Romeo of the piece, who has neglected his gang for a month, makes his first appearance — just as Romeo does in Shakespeare's second scene — and is stirred by a presentiment: "There's something due any day," "there's a miracle due," "Something's coming, something good." Where Romeo is lovesick for his Rosaline (whom we never meet), clean-cut Tony has no specific girl in mind. Without waiting for his two central protagonists to meet and woo each other, as Shakespeare's lovers do in ornamental sonnets, Laurents gives Tony his moment of lyrical self-expression, although it is fair to say that Stephen Sondheim's lyrics are too weak and colloquial to generate power and transcendent beauty. In one sense, this does not do violence to Shakespeare, for Romeo before the Capulet ball uses lumbering puns and has a soul of lead. According to Mahood, he is "too bound to earth to bound, too sore from Cupid's darts to soar in the dance." Tony, in contrast, tries to soar but he can not formulate any precise image of what is supposed to be coming his way. In other words, his lyrical impulse lacks a well-articulated motive and object.

He has not even met Maria yet, he has been bad-mouthed by fellow gang members for having been absent, and yet he senses exultantly that something great is just "around the corner, / Or whistling down the river." He lacks what T.S. Eliot would have called an "objective correlative." And yet this impulse for surging optimism is couched in a remarkable formal symmetry, beginning with an octave and sestet (a Petrarchan sonnet convention), with careful double stresses in each line, and then leading into a second sonnet of sixteen lines, with two sestets and a quatrain. The final section is apparently an incomplete sonnet, with a falling cadence that never really ends but simply fades out as if interminably.

Like Juliet, Maria makes her first appearance in the third scene. She is seen in a bridal shop, where Anita is fitting the excited girl for a big dance that night. Where Juliet has her Nurse in attendance and has to listen to Lady Capulet and the Nurse extolling Paris' virtues as a prospective bridegroom, Maria has her brother's flashy girlfriend as a chaperone. Like Juliet's Nurse, Anita is *"knowing, sexual, sharp."* And Maria recoils from the prospect of marrying Chino, just as Juliet rejects Paris. Like her Shakespearean counterpart, Maria is designated in the script as being *"an excited, enthusiastic"* child with the *"temper"* of a woman. Newly arrived in the country, she looks upon this time of her life as "the real beginning" of a young American lady. She is not yet marked by amorous passion or the wish fulfillment of any *Liebestod* myth. Where Juliet becomes absorbed and finally destroyed by a religion and madness of love, the first significant ritual for Maria is a desacralizing one, for Anita remakes a communion dress into a party dress for the upcoming dance. The profane appears to have displaced the religious, although subsequent events will show us a Maria who believes in votive prayer and forgiveness.

After the introduction of the two central lovers, the play moves on to the dance, where, after Riff has persuaded Tony to help in a rumble, dress colours (rather than masks or vizards) define the two warring sides. Once again, Laurents avoids tapestries of gorgeous language in his dramatization. Where Shakespeare leads up to Romeo and Juliet's first encounter with rough, bawdy badinage among Romeo, Mercutio, and Benvolio, culminating in Mercutio's glorious, spontaneous fantasia on Queen Mab, there is no such sportive wit in *West Side Story*. Dance and gesture replace language in ritualizing the conflicts and supplying the necessary tender sensuousness for Tony and Maria's first meeting. Dance, at first, is dramatic challenge as both the Jets and the Sharks jitterbug wildly while their faces remain *"cool, almost detached."* Perhaps this detail is Laurents' analogue for Shakespeare's masks. The recalcitrant youths put aside their hostilities only temporarily when Glad Hand, the eager "square" social director, tries to draw them together. The changes in music and movement (from jitterbug to promenade to mambo to cha-cha to dreamlike duet) lead to the hero and heroine's simultaneous, reciprocal attraction, which itself takes the form of a stylized dance, melting gang loyalties in favour of an absorbing and total focus on each other. Time, place, and ethnic hostility fade in the magic instant, and the two touch each other's faces in their version of Romeo and Juliet's "palm to palm" in "holy palmer's kiss" (1.5.98). The song "Maria" substitutes for Shakespeare's sonnets, and Sondheim's lyrics contract the lovers with an ardour that has overtones of the religion of love: "Maria! / Say it loud and there's music playing — / Say it soft and it's almost like praying — ."

And yet, even this moment relies more on feeling and echo (the word "Maria" reverberates like a tritonal set of chimes) than on elaborations of diction, imagery, and metre. Where Juliet indulges in love-idolatry that has nothing to do with her beloved's family name ("What's in a name?" — 2.2.43), Tony is totally enchanted by the sound of Maria's name, for it is "All the beautiful sounds of the world in a single word." It is his demotic form of courtly love, and a tender one devoid of adult aggressiveness; the raptness of that love helps us share a moment that cannot be reckoned by a clock or the colours of rival gangs. The counterpoint of the scene is sustained as Tony moves towards his love against the discordant hate and rage of Chino and Bernardo. As the rival gang leaders prepare for a war council at Doc's drugstore, and appeal to their girls to leave, Tony and Maria sing in counterpoint, their feeling swelling in intensity. It is as if we need to be reminded of the social and ethnic strife before we hear Tony and Maria declare the perfect harmony of their feelings for each other. The world, indeed, "will never be the same" to either again.

Shakespeare's famous balcony scene, in which Romeo stellifies Juliet and rhapsodizes her (sometimes in lushly hyperbolic language), finds a contemporary form on a fire escape overlooking a back alley. As music plays beneath most of the scene, Tony urges Maria to come down to him, but she is worried that her brother Bernardo might return home soon with Anita. What is still, of course, very much in play is the festering ethnic and racial tension between the rival gangs, for instead of exchanging the sort of highly charged romantic poetry that Shakespeare puts in the mouths of his lovers, Tony and Maria express a sensual urgency and fear of gang animosity. Their meeting is dangerous because each is "one of them" — the enemy — although the lovers wish earnestly to divorce themselves from the virulent attitudes that would force them to be afraid of each other. The situation is charged with anomalous feelings, but Laurents' dialogue is wracked by a staccato rhythm that is inappropriate to an erotic tone, and probably accounts, in part, for the inability of Stephen Sondheim to transcend the prose in favour of a soaring duet. The ballad "Tonight" becomes a love duet marred by tonal inconsistency and clichéd imagery. It begins as virtually a form of classical operetta (such as would have been sung by Nelson Eddy and Jeannette Macdonald or by Alfred Drake and Patricia Morison), and it strains after a sort of diction that would accord with ecstatic or rapturous feeling. Maria sings of the world's passing away and of Tony's becoming her whole world: "There's only you tonight, / What you are, what you do, what you say." Tony responds with a stellified image of the world and the feeling of a miracle. But when the two join in unison, they sound like two desperate lovers in a terrible Hollywood musical which is full of clumsy lyrics and leaden phrasings: "Tonight, tonight, / The world is full of light, / With suns and moons all over the place." Obviously, no finite mind could ever encompass "all over the place." Nor could any romantic fervour be secured by such subsequent lines as: "Today the world was just an address, / A place for me to live in, / No better than all right." It is difficult to believe that these are lines composed by Sondheim, for they betray an immaturity of idea and imagery.

It is clear that underlying distress of mind cannot be assuaged as yet in the story, for Tony and Maria both know that whatever their feelings for each other, they are subject to the edicts of their warring gangs. "They are strict with me," complains Maria, who hurriedly proposes that Tony meet her at the bridal shop where she works. It is here that the celebrated cult of love as religion and tragic desire finds explicit expression. The pair pronounce their mutual adoration in an identical phrase ("Te adoro"), and the site of their planned assignation anticipates a wedding in woe.

The mood changes abruptly with the arrival of the Sharks and their girls. Anita champions Maria in her plea for more freedom, but does so in a manner that relates sociology to tragedy. The villain in this story is fear, but it is fear based on the social character of American society. The two gangs typify primitive polarities of feeling and attitude in matters of identity, territory, and power, and Anita, who shares her gang's animosity towards "white" America, satirizes the American myth of generosity and tolerance and the American dream of materialistic prosperity. She clashes with Bernardo on the issue of a woman's place in the social scheme, as well as with the not-too-bright Rosalia who is nostalgic for Puerto Rico. Anita belongs to the gang, but will not accept its double standard for the two sexes. Her stichomythic exchanges with Rosalia are phrased in a hot Latin song-and-dance number that ends in raucous festivity. The whole sequence affects the audience rather than the characters, and reminds us of the ironic side of the story and of its ability to turn some of its own dark aspects into comedy with flair.

But the dark sides reappear in the next scene, set at midnight in Doc's "run-down, musty" drugstore. The much-anticipated war council provokes tension, which Riff attempts to allay with "cool" poise and authority. Where Friar Laurence chides Romeo for fickleness in affairs of the heart, Doc criticizes the Jets for racism and for making war over "a little piece of the street." Where Friar Laurence dispenses remedies for Romeo's ills, Doc dispenses sober criticism, but he is unable to quell the gang's energy, which gushes out in Riff's song "Cool," with its street vernacular and quaint slang: "Got a rocket in your pocket — Keep coolly cool, boy! . . . Take it slow and, Daddy-o, You can live it up and die in bed!" This leads into *"a frenetic dance in which the boys and girls release their emotions and get 'cool.' "* Riff challenges Bernardo to a rumble, but proceedings are interrupted by Lieutenant Schrank, who speaks a very tough language to the gangs. Ironically, he is no fitting representative of the law, for he is a racist who indulges in vile insults and slurs, and who deserves the mocking, sardonic jazz licks that follow Bernardo's whistled version of "My Country 'Tis of Thee." But he does typify an older generation out of sorts with the younger, more anarchic one. The scene ends on an even darker note with Doc's admission: "I'm frightened enough for both [gangs]."

The rumble is very much on Maria's mind — even in the bridal shop, which is the setting for Scene 7. Anita is less perturbed, for she views the upcoming fight the same way as she sees the gangs' dances — a way "to get rid of something quick." In other words, both dancing and fighting stem from youthful excesses of spirit and energy. Sex and violence are intertwined for Anita — just as they are for the boys in the line "rocket in your pocket" — for she speaks admiringly of Bernardo's healthy body and energy, and in so doing celebrates her own carnal desire. Yet, Anita is not oblivious to the danger that Maria is in for having fallen in love with a man from the wrong side. Tony's appearance relieves some of the simmering undercurrents of tension, for he speaks to Maria in extremely romantic, albeit naive, terms of magic transcendentalism: "We're untouchable; we *are* in the air; we have magic!" Maria reminds him that "Magic is also evil and black" and appeals to him to stop the scheduled rumble. She is a foil to his immature optimism, but she is so ardently in love with him that she joins in his play-acting of a marriage ceremony with two dress dummies. Slowly, seriously, this charade vanishes as the two lovers enact a wedding ceremony for themselves, without benefit of a minister, and the scene concludes with a tender duet, "One Hand, One Heart," in which the two vow that "Even death won't part us now." They kneel before an imaginary altar, and their serious exchange of vows is a ritual witnessed by the dummies in the shop. Tony and Maria both know that their desire conflicts with reality, and this knowledge brings a tender ruefulness that accords with a story of youth, love, and impending doom. With their ceremony, the young lovers prompt us to remember many of the great stories of young lovers doomed by fate and family hostility. But Laurents' lovers do not *elect* death, though they do seek the satisfaction of their forbidden desires, and so place themselves at the mercy of circumstance and environment. In other words, there is no clear death wish, and it is anachronistic to align this play with pure classical myths. What exists palpably under the scene, however, is the feeling that Tony and Maria are "wedded to calamity" — as Friar Laurence remarked of Romeo (3.3.3).

The touching abstractness in this scene leads to a wholly musical scene in which all the characters appear separately, against small sets representing different places in the neighbourhood. *"All are waiting expectantly for the coming of night, but for very different reasons."* Both gangs sing of going to have their way that night, and the sharp, strident counterpoints yoke together their violent passions. Different motifs are forced together: the gangs sing of the fight; Anita of lust; Tony and Maria of love and the transformation of nature. In effect, there is a dazzling vocal kaleidoscope, with snatches of verse from previous songs, reprises of choruses, and fresh lyrics that build with the music to an exultant but somewhat dissonant climax and blackout. What comes to mind is Shakespeare's line: "These violent delights have violent ends, / And in their triumph die" (2.6.9–10).

The dramatic climax, however, is reached in the next scene, under the highway, as the almost-silhouetted gangs enter from separate sides by climbing over fences or crawling through holes in the walls. It is now 9 p.m. and after the eight preceding scenes — all of which are set at early evening or night or midnight — it becomes clear that, as in *Romeo and Juliet*, the one character we hardly ever see is the sun. There are, of course, numerous light and dark contrasts in the play, but all the action occurs in fading light or penumbral darkness. This temporal quality carries us (without our necessarily being aware) into dark moods engendered by dreams or irrational and absurd convictions, and into shocking developments that heighten the fateful character of the story.

Bernardo is supposed to fight Diesel, but taunts Tony so mercilessly that Riff reacts spontaneously and violently, thereby propelling himself into a fight against Bernardo. This becomes a form of dance, with the two antagonists jockeying for position, feinting, duelling. Just as Riff has his opportunity to kill Bernardo, Tony breaks free from Diesel's grasp and cries out to Riff to stop. The moment is enough for Bernardo to stab Riff. Events rapidly grow chaotic. Tony leaps forward to catch Riff as the victim falls, then seizes the knife, and leaps at Bernardo. A free-for-all breaks out and, in the confusion, Tony kills Bernardo. The violence is choreographed to a musical passage lasting about two and a half minutes, and it is stopped only by a sharp police whistle as the youths waver and dispel in panic. As the stage clears, Tony is seen standing in horror over the bodies of Riff and Bernardo. He bends over them, stares, then cries out Maria's name in anguish. Anybodys, the anxious, scrawny teenager, appears out of the shadows and tugs at Tony insistently. He realizes the danger he is in and flees with her to an escapeway. She disappears just as he is almost trapped by a searchlight. However, he manages to get away as a distant clock begins to boom, and he becomes, like Romeo, a fugitive from the law.

This summary reveals the non-literary appeal of the script. The climax is almost totally dependent on movement, body language, lighting, and sound effects. Unlike the fatal duels in Shakespeare, where accidental deaths are framed by effectively ironic speeches (think of Mercutio's "A plague on both your houses" — 3.1.96), Laurents' characters are largely inarticulate and unable to rise above crudely aggressive mockery or provocation. Now this is not fundamentally at odds with the Shakespearean source, for Shakespeare often uses prose that is demotic and comical for certain characters. The absence of embroidered language allows for action and a direct language of movement. Laurents' characters make their bodies and actions speak for them, but as the police whistle and booming clock show, the play is not tragic because of Tony's love for Maria, but because of the circumscription of the two lovers by time and environment. The pair live in the wrong time and in the wrong place, rather like Romeo and Juliet, who are caught in the midst of a raging family feud that feeds its own appetite with several lives.

West Side Story has no deep psychological content as a tragedy. But, then, neither does Romeo and Juliet which, as John Wain contends, makes an impression of "pure pathos." Wain sketches how Romeo and Juliet "is in essence a comedy that turns out tragically," because it begins with materials for comedy — "the stupid parental generation, the instant attraction of the young lovers, the quick surface life of street fights, masked balls and comic servants" — but then this material is blighted as the gaiety and good fortune are drained away. In other words, it "does not build with inherently tragic materials."

In West Side Story, so far, there is little comic material, and what there is is crude, naive, cynical, and aggressive. Most of the plot is feud-ridden. Tony and Maria wish to escape from this world, but they have no apparent substitute for it. At least Romeo and Juliet have the prospect of Padua, and by travelling there from Verona, they could be apart from any other Capulet or Montague. But in West Side Story, there is no such respite.

Act Two begins ironically, for it is set in a bedroom where gay music accompanies Consuelo's self-examination in a mirror, Rosalia's manicure, and Maria's rushed costuming. This makes for a light-hearted feminine spirit, as Maria eagerly anticipates her wedding night. She thinks that the rumble has been called-off, and in her rapture she sings "I Feel Pretty," a ballad that is beautiful in itself but totally out of character. The first three lines alone are enough to convince us that they would be more suited to Eliza Doolittle than to the Latin heroine: "I feel pretty, / Oh, so pretty, / I feel pretty, and witty and bright." The phrasing is elegant and the rhyming clever — with some deft internal rhymes — and the total impression created is of a young woman with European, rather than Puerto Rican, sophistication: "I feel charming, / Oh, so charming — / It's alarming how charming I feel." And with the vocal accompaniment of Rosalia and Consuelo, the number becomes a sweet delight that has nothing to do with the girls' personalities.

But just as the song begins to be an incongruous distraction, Chino enters to report that Tony has killed Bernardo. The wording he uses ("Nobody meant for it to happen . . .") points up the accidental or arbitrary nature of tragic circumstance. The issue is one of emotion rather than of ideology. Maria's reaction is instantaneous, vehement, and marked by agitated conflicts of feeling. Her first impulse is one of shocked denial ("You are lying!"), then she breaks into a form of religious fervour as she kneels before her domestic shrine and rocks back and forth in a prayer that is schizoid in its broken mixture of Spanish and English. Here she becomes imploring ("Make it not be true . . . please make it not be true"), but when Tony quietly climbs into the room from the fire-escape window, she is torn between denunciatory rage and tearful love. They are both emotionally vulnerable. Tony offers an agonized recounting of the fatal events, and offers to give himself up to the police. But Maria's bitterness melts into forgiveness, and the two lovers repeat their desire to find some refuge from the corruption around them. Maria's assertion of an external force that is responsible for shaping events plainly repeats the idea, well developed in Shakespeare, that though love is a mighty power, destiny or simply the external world is mightier still and often cruel:

TONY: We'll be all right. I know it. We're really together now.
MARIA: But it's not us! It's everything around us!
TONY: Then we'll find some place where nothing can get to us; not one of them, not anything.

Tony expands their wish-fulfillment fantasy into the opening verse for "Somewhere," which is sung as a dream ballad and accompanied by a ballet. As he sings, *"the walls of the apartment begin to move off, and the city walls surrounding them begin to close in on them."* Then choreography becomes highly expressive of the intrinsic drama behind the emotions: *"the two lovers begin to run, battering against the walls of the city, beginning to break through as chaotic figures of the gangs, of violence, flail around them."* They do break through, and suddenly they are in a purer world — one of *"space, air, and sun."*

This startling transition to a sun-basked innocence in soft pastel colours produces a mood of warm joy. This is the first time that we actually see the sun in the story, and this "miracle" is celebrated by a gentle love dance to an offstage female voice's singing of "Somewhere." The particular lyric of this song articulates the lovers' optimistic belief that they will find "a new way of living" and "a way of forgiving," but the very fact that there is as yet no identifiable place or time for such a blessed existence imbues the dream moment with poignancy. Just as the lovers succeed in prompting the rival gangs to join hands in a winding procession through a *"would-be world,"* there is *"a dead stop." "The harsh shadows, the fire escapes of the real, tenement world cloud the sky, and the figures of* RIFF *and* BERNARDO *slowly walk on. The dream becomes a nightmare: as the city returns, there are brief re-enactments of the knife fight, of the deaths. Maria and Tony are once again separated from each other by the violent warring. . . . They can not reach each other."* There is chaotic confusion and blackness before *"they find themselves back in the bedroom, clinging to each other desperately. . . ."*

The abstract, serious, touching temper of this scene yields to comic relief in the next, for as Officer Krupke enters an alley to question the Jets about Tony's whereabouts, they elude him and then regroup for a song that satirizes social clichés of American family life and the roots of juvenile delinquency: "It's just our bringin'upke / That gets us out of hand, / Our mothers all are junkies, / Our fathers all are drunks." The tone is flippant, with some comic-strip expressions, but all-too-knowing as the Jets make deliberate sport of their own purported psychological neuroses and society's anxious prescriptions. They sing mockingly of being depraved because they are deprived, and they concoct a risible list of social clichés that run the gamut from the mundane to the absurd:

My father is a bastard,
My ma's an S.O.B.
My grandpa's always plastered,
My grandma pushes tea.
My sister wears a mustache,

My brother wears a dress.
Goodness gracious, that's why I'm a mess!

Fully aware of the truism that juvenile delinquency is "a social disease," they target all the familiar generalizations of social workers, analysts, and other establishment figures in order to glorify their own anti social behaviour.

To some people this scene may seem gratuitously out of character with the rest of the story, but the seeds of its anarchic comedy were already present in the first scene of the play in the "Jet Song," which celebrated gang brotherhood and gang life. Moreover, *West Side Story* is less about Tony and Maria than about the forces that crush young love and the chance of a non-cynical life. The comic tone of "Gee, Officer Krupke" amplifies the insolence of hotheaded youth that has been responsible for perverse, devastating events. The gangs are choruses who show up society's futility in attempting to pit reason against primitive urges and acts. As such, even their satiric song serves a dramatic function, for their violent ecstasies in being beyond social understanding and acceptance show how easy it is for events to mount rapidly beyond anyone's ordered control. Their song and behaviour compound the burden of the story, which is emotional rather than idealistic, and the scene ends on a different note as the Jets decide to look for Tony because they fear that Chino will kill him.

The final four scenes alternate between private and public settings as the pity and terror increase. The rapid action and pressing gloom are concentrations of a tragic sense, but before the final rush of events, there is an emotional scene between Maria and Anita, in which some of the most violent dialectics are crystallized in a song of intense counterpoint. This scene is set only a half-hour before midnight in Maria's bedroom, where Tony and Maria lie together in a vague glow. With Anita's sudden entrance, the quiet ecstasy is shattered. To Anita, Tony is the enemy — a boy who has killed Maria's own brother and who will murder Maria's love just as he has murdered Anita's. Her song is bitterly savage in tone and marked by staccato rhythms. Maria sings her denial in counterpoint ("It's true

for you, not for me") and immediately summarizes the whole conflict between head and heart. Her heart, it is clear, does not seek
reasons for loving. It simply does not wish to know. "I love him; I'm
his, / And everything he is / I am, too." Obviously captivated by the
miraculous splendour of love, she has abandoned herself totally to
romantic feeling. Love has become her life, and she and Anita finally
converge in a chorus that enunciates how love cancels all moral
distinctions between right and wrong.

This is the last meditation on the nature and consequences of love
before the upsurge in action. Before the bedroom scene ends,
Schrank enters to question Maria. Complaining of a headache, Maria
asks Anita to go to the drugstore to tell Doc to hold the "medicine"
there until she can fetch it herself. This is a privately coded message,
of course, for the "medicine" is Tony. She then gives false information to Schrank about the rumble, and a mood of forbidding gloom
begins to gather strength.

The "medicine" at Doc's is another obvious link to Shakespeare,
for in *Romeo and Juliet* Friar Laurence gives Juliet a potion with which
to feign death. Shakespeare's is a short scene of merely 126 lines, and
is marked by an exchange between a grieving Juliet and an impor-
tunate Paris who still would like to compel her to love him. Laurents'
scene is even shorter in dialogue (by almost a half), but it is incarnate
with violent passions as Anita arrives to deliver Maria's message
while Tony is hiding out in the basement. She can not convince the
Jets that she wants to stop Chino and save Tony, and she is subjected
to vile personal and racial abuse. *"The taunting breaks out into a wild,
savage dance, with epithets hurled at* ANITA, *who is encircled and driven
by the whole pack."* She is in mortal danger of being raped and is saved
only by Doc's timely entrance. Unlike Friar Laurence, Doc does not
have a truly active role in the plot, but he does serve as *vox Americana*.
Anita bitterly adds a catalyst to the rush of events by blurting out,
"Tell the murderer Maria's *never* going to meet him! Tell him Chino
found out — and shot her!"

The taunting, near-rape, and Anita's vile lie fortify the emotional
underpinnings of the play, and show that this is not a work of probes
the mystery of life. It is a play about conditioned responses and

provocations. Even Doc's angry disgust shows that the characters do not understand either the forces that have contaminated them or their own irrational deviancy. "What does it take to get through to you? When do you stop? *You make this world lousy!*" The final sentence here draws attention to the atmosphere of the story. Laurents' libretto has made it amply clear that Maria and Tony are not poet-lovers, born of leisure and the romantic imagination. The starkly stripped-down language, the absence of artful phrases, the brief scenes, and the expressive dances unite to create a stirring design of accident and catastrophe. Love is seen in a distorted glass, as it were, and as yet has not produced an irreversible transformation of soul. Love is circumscribed by the wild impetuosities of youth and by overwhelming discouragement.

The penultimate scene is the shortest in the play, consisting of a mere twenty-one lines of dialogue. It occurs in the drugstore cellar (a rough equivalent for the vault in Shakespeare) and is set about ten minutes before midnight. Doc attempts literally to slap Tony into an awareness of the gangs' destructiveness. "Why do you live like there's a war on? Why do you kill?" he questions impassionedly, sounding like a choric voice of mainstream America. Tony is still too dazed by the brief splendour of his love for Maria to heed Doc's words, but when Doc reports what Anita has said in the earlier scene, Tony is benumbed with shock and rushes out into the darkness, yelling, "Chino? *Chino?* Come and get me, too, Chino."

The final climax occurs, fittingly, at midnight and in a street — with both time and locale being emblematic of forces that impinge upon the characters. Midnight is the witching hour, when black magic and evil can have full reign, but, more fundamentally, night and darkness signify death and the unconscious. The open street, the same as at the beginning of Act One, is an intermediate zone, as it were, between order and chaos. *"Jagged with shadows"* (as the stage directions say), it is empty before Tony's entrance. On the simplest level, it is an emblem of the territorial imperative, for it is a place that each of the rival gangs wishes to appropriate fully for itself. Since it is also the site of battle, it is emblematic of chaos and the possible. Tony has obviously emerged from underground (the cellar) into an open, empty, dark space. But he is only on middle ground, so to speak. There is yet the sky above.

With such symbolism vibrating within the scene, Tony yells out for Chino, urging him to appear for their showdown. Suddenly he sees Maria, and as they run desperately to each other, a gun shot rings out from Chino and Tony falls. The bitter-sweet moment is heightened by the lovers' final dialogue and Maria's refrain from "Somewhere":

MARIA: Loving is enough.
TONY: Not here. They won't let us be.
MARIA: Then we'll get away.
TONY: Yes, we can. We *will*.

As from the outset of their sudden discovery of love, the two wish to be left to themselves, free to love without constraints of gang loyalty or racial considerations. Maria sings to him, and as he starts to join in, she sings harder as if to urge him back to life, but he falters and dies. Her song is a poignant reminder that their earlier music together was an attempt to escape to another world, and the incompleteness of the final ballad intensifies their loneliness and separateness from others.

Shakespeare's tragedy culminates in secular ritual. In its final scene — which is much longer than Laurents' — Paris enters the Capulet tomb with his page, who bears flowers and a torch. Grief-stricken Romeo forces open the tomb and offers to join Juliet in death. Then he duels with and kills Paris, before drinking the fatal potion. Friar Laurence fails to stop Juliet's suicide, and there is next some business with servants who gather in a tableau of grief as Prince Escalus and Lord and Lady Capulet enter with others for their exclamations of woe. The Montagues appear too, and the play ends with obsequies and Escalus' solemn finale about "a glooming peace" when "some shall be pardon'd and some punished" (5.3.304–307). Much, of course, depends on a stage director's skill in extending the scene with a slow procession and off-stage singing, and on a final moving tableau with the two feuding families finally worn out and reconciled. Yet, such an ending, even with impressive staging, would seem like an empty spectacle without a palpable sense of tragic equilibrium. As John Russell Brown contends: "Shakespeare's complicated last movement of the tragedy shows that however powerful destiny may seem, men and a Prince among men react to catastrophe first in guilt . . . and then with a sifting of responsibility and a demand for justice."

West Side Story also concludes with secular ritual and an attempt to achieve an equilibrium. As the orchestra finishes the last bars of "Somewhere," Maria gently rests Tony on the ground, lightly brushes his lips with her fingers, and then in savage rage challenges Chino and the two gangs with a gun. Her theme is one of common guilt: "WE ALL KILLED HIM; and my brother and Riff. I, too. I CAN KILL NOW BECAUSE I HATE NOW." But despite pointing the weapon wildly, she cannot fire, breaks into tears, hurls the gun away, and sinks to the ground. When Schrank enters and moves toward Tony's body, Maria becomes madly protective, racing to the body and embracing it feverishly, refusing to allow Schrank to touch it. Krupke and Glad Hand appear and remain in shadow, but then there is a transformation. Maria turns and looks at Chino, holding out her arms to him. When he responds by slowly standing by the body, she repeats the gesture for Action and Diesel, then Pepe joins Chino, and Maria leans over Tony's face, whispering the words they had once woven into a solemn promise to each other: "Te adoro." The final action is pure ritual: music starts as two members from each gang lift Tony's body, and all other members form a procession — a mirror, as it were, of the very procession they had made in the dream ballet of the opening scene of Act Two. Baby John picks up Maria's shawl and places it over her head, and she sits quietly, *"like a woman in mourning,"* as the music builds, the lights come up, and the procession moves across the stage. At last, she rises, and with a proud lift of her head, she follows the others, as the adults — Doc, Schrank, Krupke, and Glad Hand — are left *"bowed, alone, useless."*

This conclusion makes several statements through its imagery and choreography, and they all coalesce around the figure of Maria. The religious significance of her name is underscored in the final sequence, for she becomes both grieving Madonna and mother of both gangs whom she binds, too late, in a melancholy union. And when the lights come up, though it is far from daylight, there is a promise of a more peaceable time and way of life. She has shown how effectively the night is related to the feminine principle, but far from being a passive emblem of potentiality and hope, Maria is the most active figure on stage, ensuring by the ritualistic procession for her dead lover that the night is a kind of journey from a spiritual hell to a resurrection of sorts. Tony is dead, but his love for Maria has passed into mythology, because as he is borne aloft and off stage, the procession is a brief pilgrimage that indicates a collective journey away from a dominion of destructiveness to a time and world less contaminated by savage passions.

The question is whether Maria is a convincing embodiment of this miraculous change. From the outset, she is never the pure child, blessedly free from worldly matters. Her first appearance in the play makes the impression of an extremely lovely, young girl who is excited about the dance in the gym and about being in America. True, these are not profound issues, but she makes her feelings plain. She wants a sexier dress, and one with some showy colour. She is uninspired by Chino and chafes at having to be subject to her brother's will. And though she falls head over heels for Tony, her love cuts through categories of gang loyalty and race. She does not see Tony simply as a white boy, a Jet, or the enemy — she sees a person. But she is always aware of the extreme social and emotional conflicts her forbidden love arouses. She stands in opposition to gang attitudes and to the irrational fear that feeds on a clan's hostilities, and it is she who prompts Tony to try and stop the rumble, and who supports him when he is afraid in Act Two. In short, her psychology has the seeds of mature growth and fruition, though Arthur Laurents does not grant her the linguistic eloquence she would need to decorate her own development rhetorically. Where Shakespeare's Juliet has a notoriously difficult task in managing the often high-flown verse, Maria has the unenviable task of appearing to be fully fleshed despite a deficiency of spoken text. Maria is forced to be dramatically effective through her imagination, which is only experienced through her songs and choreographed movements. Somehow she has to draw upon resources of her innermost self in order to kill every emotion (except love) within herself. And this love is required to be an exalting, transcendental passion that survives the deaths of Bernardo, Riff, and Tony to grow beyond narrow personal desires to a redemptive state.

But the intrinsic problem in this pattern is that *West Side Story* has not prepared a vivid case for this ultimate change in emotion and thought. Good drama makes directness, rapidity, and shape of presentation serve the ends simultaneously of concentration and probability. Melodrama, on the other hand (in the words of Una Ellis-Fermor), "fails to integrate passion and event by thought, and lacks in general that depth of imagination upon which the revelation of character and emotion depend." *West Side Story* is more melodrama than tragedy or even good drama: there isn't enough of a balance of contrary experiences — a balance between the malevolent gangs and a patterned world (society). Its conclusion with Maria's remedy is too suddenly made to be a convincing form of overruling good. Certainly, there is no denying its simultaneous pain and exaltation, but it fails to define from the first the inner life of its heroine, and so the final goodness seems ordained by the playwright's urge to be moralistic and sane. The remedy to mindless violence is imposed by a playwright's mind that wishes social readjustments, and so it fails to do justice to the fundamental nature of evil or casual suffering. Despite the numb bewilderment of the young characters, the futile presence of the adults, and the painful destruction in the scene, the play is finally social propaganda rather than true tragedy.

FIGURE 2

Leonard Bernstein and Jerome Robbins.

PHOTO: FRIEDMAN ABELES

ALL PHOTOS (EXCEPT FIGURE 15) COURTESY OF
THE NEW YORK PUBLIC LIBRARY FOR THE PERFORMING ARTS

FIGURE 3
Larry Kert and Carol Lawrence.
PHOTO: FRIEDMAN ABELES

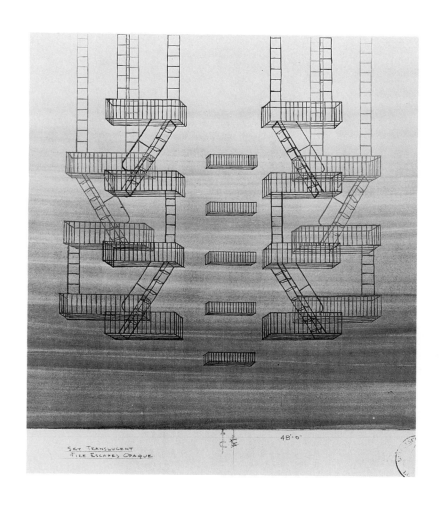

FIGURE 4

Oliver Smith's design of the fire escapes.

PHOTO: VANDAMM

FIGURE 5

Oliver Smith's design of the drugstore.

PHOTO: VANDAMM

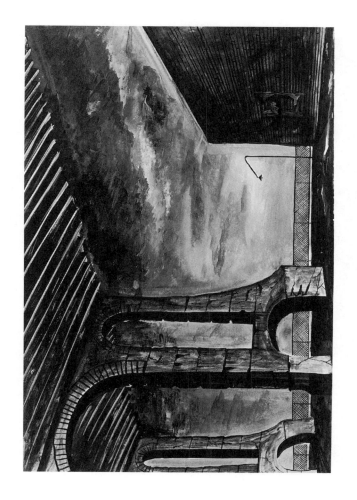

FIGURE 6

Oliver Smith's design for the rumble at night.

PHOTO: VANDAMM

FIGURE 7

Three of the Jets (from the 1959 production at the Winter Garden).

PHOTO: VANDAMM

FIGURE 8

"Gee, Officer Krupke."

PHOTO: FRED FEHL

FIGURE 9

Drugstore dance.

PHOTO: FRED FEHL

FIGURE 10

Anybodys looks forlorn.

PHOTO: FRED FEHL

FIGURE II

Jive sequence from "The Dance at the Gym."

PHOTO: FRED FEHL

FIGURE 12

The Sharks' girls (from the 1959 production at the Winter Garden).

PHOTO: VANDAMM

FIGURE 13

Mambo sequence from "The Dance at the Gym."

PHOTO: FRED FEHL

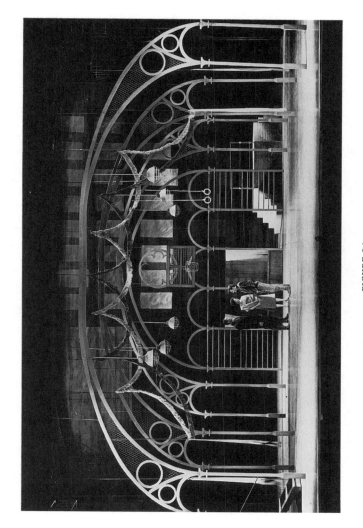

FIGURE 14

A quiet trio in the gym.

PHOTO: VANDAMM

FIGURE 15

Maria.

PHOTO: WILL RAPPORT

COURTESY OF THE HARVARD THEATER COLLECTION

FIGURE 16
"One Hand, One Heart" in the Bridal Shop.
PHOTO: FRED FEHL

FIGURE 17
"A Boy like That."

PHOTO: FRED FEHL

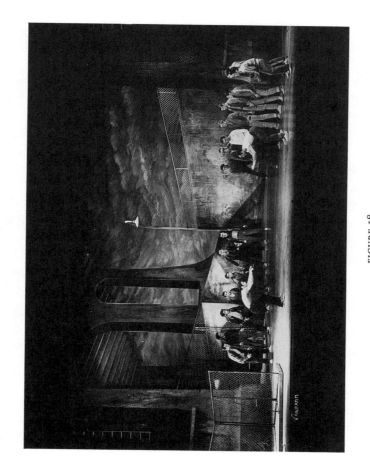

FIGURE 18

The rumble.

PHOTO: VANDAMM

Bernstein's Musical Drama

BERNSTEIN'S SCORE COMPLETES what Laurents' libretto sketches out as drama. Bernstein here is very much a co-dramatist, for his music expands the situations to make its own drama, combining the abstract and the concrete, and catalyzing emotional states or shades.

The score of *West Side Story* thoroughly integrates motifs and themes, and shows an impressive array of musical elements that are cleverly linked together throughout the show. In the view of Joseph P. Swain, the "Prologue" is "the source of all Bernstein's important musical elements." It opens, as Swain shows, with a mixture of major and minor chords and a blues sound. Next, the tritone is heard, with sharp clashes in tone and pitch, thereby creating a polytonal texture which is dominated by a key of C. In layman's terms, the first chord is high and followed by short, sharp beats, syncopated with finger snapping, and leading to a lush brass and string passage. But the sharp, staccato accents dominate, especially as they are accompanied by sinister drums. There is a rising cadence with some dramatic pauses and then the bongo drums gain tempo and rhythm, compounded by brass instruments and gang whistlings. The jazz rhythm begins to race, growing frenetic, with pulsing, throbbing, polytonal measures and emphatic chords. This builds musical tension and a mood of roughness — both highly appropriate to the expository mimed dance through which the audience first meets the rival gangs and recognizes their distinctive personalities.

There is no technical break between the "Prologue" and the "Jet Song," for motifs from the first musical number still play under the lyric of the gang's song. Some passages are clear repetitions of the first musical line of the "Prologue," although here they sound cruder and lead to a quick crescendo before the whole song really ends. The rushed, driving beat builds with an energy that summarizes the image of a group of restless youths, as the tone clusters stamp the music with an undeniably American quality.

Bernstein's technical ability glows in "Something's Coming," Tony's first vocal rendition and a solo that has musical elements already heard in the previous numbers. The key, however, is different, perhaps because Tony is one of the doomed protagonists and, so, needs a special pitch that will underline his feeling of breathless expectancy. The song ends on an endlessly lowered note to enforce this feeling and shade it with mystery.

The score connects its own parts in long chains. The "Prologue" is a musical paradigm which feeds into the entire score and leads directly to the "Jet Song." Then in the middle of the "Jet Song" comes a tune that will later be the opening stage-band melody in "The Dance at the Gym."

The bongos, strings, and brass strike up mambo chords for the gym dance, with the bongos actually repeating tones and rhythms from the "Prologue" and "Jet Song." It is all very hot and Latin, with force and flair that dramatize a flamboyant display of power by the two gangs. After the lovers see each other during this wild dance, the music alters. A delicate "Cha-Cha" begins in a new key, and Tony and Maria slowly drift into an intimate but dream-like dance. This transition leads to Tony's full-voiced expression of transforming love in "Maria." This is an important song lyrically, dramatically, and musically, because it expresses love in a tense situation. Bernstein is compelled to express this love and some sense of the helplessness of the two lovers given over to a powerful passion in the face of gang hostility. But the song is not marked by a single mood. It encompasses Tony's dazed amazement, his bewilderment and full-blown rapture, as well as a helpless utterance that (as Swain says) "can do nothing but name its cause." The music accelerates into full-scale melody, mixing Latin and jazz notes. The high point is a rhapsodic counterpoint, and the song concludes with a repetition of Maria's name and a dying cadence that echoes the one in "Something's Coming."

Bernstein's musical structure is built from what Swain calls "continuous musical sequences." The first of these reaches from the gym dance into "Maria," and ends with the "Balcony Scene." This "Balcony Scene" rings out with "Tonight." Maria sings the first verse alone in a very traditional, romantic fashion, reminiscent of classical operetta. Tony responds in duet counterpoint, and then she carries the melody upward to its culmination as a duet in unison. Strings (especially the cello) dominate the orchestral sound, and their lushness convincingly finishes the celebration of fearless love. This scene as Swain contends, enables Maria to "express her own feelings as a balance to Tony's previous song, and then to deepen and make credible the relationship itself, as does Shakespeare's balcony scene."

The second sequence is preceded by "America" and "Cool" — the first with a marimba beat, wood block, bongo, and hand-clapping accompaniment, and the second a finger-snapping number with a drum sequence growing in tempo and dissonance that is reminiscent of passages in the "Prologue." Both numbers fit comfortably within Bernstein's overall design for the show, and provide some relief before the musical sequence that includes "One Hand, One Heart," the quintet "Tonight," and "The Rumble."

"One Hand, One Heart" is sung in the bridal-shop scene, where the Polish-American Tony and the Puerto Rican Maria exchange marriage vows with sacramental solemnity and purposefulness. The song is candidly moving, and is scored predominantly for flute and strings. As Swain points out, it continues the love theme already introduced by "Maria" and "Tonight," and subtly interposes a motif from "Somewhere" (a song that is heard only in the next act) so as to hint at a profound change of mood.

But Bernstein quickly returns to dissonance, for hardly have the final *pianissimo* chords of "One Hand, One Heart" died away, than the score sounds jarring notes to the opening of the quintet "Tonight." The five principal roles in the ensemble are sung by Bernardo, Riff, Anita, Tony, and Maria, complemented by choral passages for the two gangs who, ironically, share the same music. As Swain says: "The dramatic purpose of the quintet is to present the five principal characters anticipating the coming evening in a way that summarizes their fated courses in the drama." Each principal sings a solo in the first half (except Maria), and then there is an "intensifying counterpoint on two musical themes." The Jets and Sharks both sing of going to have "their day / Tonight," and create a bitter irony, which is also shared by Anita, who modifies the lyric in her own peculiarly lusty way. This is the violent section of the song, but it is followed by Tony and Maria singing a reprise of "Tonight" from their "Balcony Scene." Bernstein does risk lessening the tension by this lyrical modulation, but cleverly controls and transforms the risk by increasing the strings' participation as double to Tony's singing. With the ensemble's rising dissonance, all the parts of the quintet come together in a resounding vocal kaleidoscope. The precise moment when the five parts join together culminates in a high C, and is (in Swain's view) "the most climactic moment in the play." The last measures of the ensemble "recall the musical premises of the 'Prologue.' " The whole piece dramatizes the intertwining of love and hate in the story, and becomes "the musical-dramatic climax of the first act and the greatest operatic ensemble ever composed for the Broadway stage."

How, then, to end the first act after such a virtuoso climax? What lyric could possibly develop from what has already been deployed in the quintet ensemble? The narrative has thrust toward a gang battle. A short dialogue under the highway precedes the rumble, but Bernstein shrewdly allows dance rather than song to complete the action. "The Rumble" music begins only after Riff strikes Bernardo with his fist for having insulted Tony. Swain claims: "The opening measures continue the development of explicit 'Prologue' material," but there is more dissonance than in the "Prologue," with thicker clusters of sound. As "The Rumble" is meant to be a fight sequence with a double killing, the music integrates the events and their mood, achieving a more frightening and powerful effect than mere words would create at this point. The choreographed violence is aided by Bernstein's dramatic music that incorporates metallic, percussive vibration and a sombre set of chimes at the end.

Act Two begins with a song, "I Feel Pretty," that is often mistaken for pure comic relief. True, it is a bedroom ballad in which Maria anticipates her wedding night, and its internal rhymes and fizzy buoyancy give it a popular show-tune quality. Moreover, with Rosalia and Consuelo's singing in operetta counterpoint and with a finish reminiscent of Rodgers and Hammerstein, it hardly appears to belong in Bernstein's score. However, it does have at least one connection with the tragic scheme because there is a double irony embedded in Maria's joyful lyrics. There are intimations that the song's surface and skipping melody should not be taken only at face value, for Maria has lines such as "It's alarming how charming I feel / And so pretty / That I hardly can believe I'm real." This lyric suggests that she is at least the tiniest bit wary of her own rapture, and that her rhapsody may well be the jubilation before catastrophe. There is an incisive irony in her own scepticism. The bedroom setting, the gay music, and the choral counterpoint are not probably meant to yield to any strong counter-feeling of doubt or apprehension, but just as Shakespeare's tragedies often present moments of sardonic black humour near the tip of a dizzying abyss, Bernstein sweeps away dramatic tension momentarily before Chino's entrance to report on the fatal rumble.

The second comic song is, indeed, more of a satiric diversion, even though it, too, has a role in Bernstein's drama. "Gee, Officer Krupke" is relatively long — compared to some of the most dramatic numbers — and has a characteristic Broadway sound that does not provoke difficult emotions. It could easily have been duplicated by any number of composers and lyricists, and as a rousing production number in which young delinquents celebrate their own anti-social behaviour it has an up-tempo quality that is rebelliously vulgar, as in the sign off: "Gee, Officer Krupke — / Krup you!" So, once again, what seems like a diversion to make an audience chuckle subverts its own humour by the implication that beneath all the flippant levity, there is an undeniable danger in the characters. Their joking is manipulative. They seem to know exactly how society would seek to explain them, and so they mock the system with its own clichés and platitudes. By this song, they perversely use society's language or catch-phrases for their own audacious ends, thereby reminding us that they will always be the enemy because their energy is so creatively rebellious.

The rest of Act Two pushes into abstraction with important dance sequences ("Ballet Sequence," "Taunting Scene," and "Finale") that integrate dramatic events with passions carried by the music. When Tony and Maria are secretly reunited after the rumble, he sings a four-line arioso, beginning "I'll take you away, take you far far away out of here," which is a transition to the "Somewhere" motif sung by an off-stage female voice. The music then modulates into a gentle love dance prior to the off-stage voice's singing of "Somewhere." Despite the fact that the lyrics are sentimental and the mood paradisiacally optimistic, the libretto and score do make a connection with tragedy by the structure of the sequence. The sequence is completed by a dream processional and nightmare re-enactment of the knife fights and deaths, where the instrumentation suits the violence. A sinister cello is struck up under the lines, as strings and piano change tone and accent into something sharp and savage, concluding with shuddering chords. Finally, there is the brief duet of Tony and Maria, whereby there is a return to the doomed-love theme.

This theme informs much of the musical articulation. There is a brief but colourful triumph of love over mindless hate in "A Boy Like That," which starts off as Anita's bitter rebuke of Maria for her relationship with Tony, only to lead to an equally dramatic denial and a final suasion by Maria. The tone clusters, tritones, and accents echo the opening measures of the "Prologue," as Anita's hatred of Tony (for having killed her beloved) is conveyed through accented offbeats ("One *of your own* kind, stick *to your own* kind!"). What is surprising is that Maria's confrontation with her repeats the same musical elements as those used by Anita. Bernstein compounds the surprise by having the two sing in parallel — with Maria asserting her devotion to Tony, and Anita reprising the chorus of savage complaint that she has just sung. Finally, this confrontation turns into something totally different when Maria begins her trope, "I have a love, and it's all that I have." No longer is Maria merely turning Anita's words back on her — as she had done with "It's true for you, not for me" — for she is now singing a different melody that becomes a persuasive expression of love. Her modulations of tone and pitch reach a crescendo, then drop for a brief duet passage with Anita, before reaching a rising final movement as both women acknowledge together that "When love comes so strong, / There is no right or wrong, / Your love is your life!"

The libretto and score progress through dance, for next comes the "Taunting Scene," which reveals what happens to Anita when she tries to deliver Maria's message to Tony, who is in hiding. The "Taunting Scene" is one of the dance sequences that narrate the story while abstracting it. Theatrical without being meretricious spectacle, it plays no role in the dénouement and resolution.

Bernstein's score works towards closure by a "Finale" that completes the lovers' story and resolves the gang warfare. "Somewhere" plays a central role here, not by being a mere reprise for sentimental reasons, but by revealing (what Swain calls) "the ultimate denial" of the lovers' simple hope. After he is shot by Chino, Tony is given his final utterance, and then Maria sings the end of the song, "picking it up," comments Swain, "at the precise spot where Tony did to rally her courage at the end of the nightmare sequence." There is no orchestral accompaniment for her voice, because she can only try to urge him back to life. The key note here is C, and Tony dies where the climax of the song should come but does not: a heartbroken Maria can not complete the melody. Instead, the orchestra does it for her. She silently entreats members of both gangs to carry Tony's body away, and the "Procession" begins like one in the earlier dream ballet, before turning into a dirge with solemn, doleful, and dignified notes. The controlling keys are still the ones that started the play, and so the dramatic closure is matched to the musical pattern.

The score has prompted Martin Gottfried to claim that *West Side Story* "will never be musically dated." The music actively expresses the action while articulating the underlying structure of incident and character. As such, it completes the presentation of the story in an immediate and powerful manner.

Symbiosis

AUDITIONS LASTED SIX MONTHS and were difficult primarily because of the special needs of the show. Robbins and his production team required new, young talent — performers who were relatively fresh on the Broadway scene and who could dance, move well, act, and sing the difficult score. The producers placed countless calls for actors, and even attempted to lure amateurs who might compensate for a lack of professional training with an innate sincerity and raw emotion bred of an authentic, working-class background. Robbins attended case-settlement houses and schools in the hope that a few youths who looked "right" might be great "discoveries." But disappointment came fast. "You never saw such frightened faces when they went on stage," he reported to Murray Schumach in the *New York Times*. Consequently, he decided to stick to big names or to littler ones, but all fresh from professional ranks. Performers were auditioned from television, movies, and stage. Nevertheless, there were some unusual auditioners. One actor was decidedly swishy in his reading and movement, but when he called up later, he sounded different on the phone — almost as if he had been playing his strange idea of a character earlier. A girl, who had a little putty nose and who wasn't very pretty close up, did a fake reading, as if she had been saturated by too much musical comedy. Even those who were good, naturalistic actors were having problems. As Robbins said: "We had good actors whose style was not right for this musical because the over-all quality is bigger than naturalness, it's higher keyed than ordinary. We tried nearly all the young actors you see in television shows about juvenile delinquency. But generally they lacked the kinetic physical energy, the ability to move, that dancers have." Schumach describes how "Robbins tested them by having them do mambo and cha-cha steps," but his problem was that of having a cast balanced in appearance and personality. "These two gangs were not just two chorus lines. We wanted great distinction of personality between members of the gangs." The crisis in casting came just before the final selection. He declared, "Let's cast with what we've got instead of waiting for perfection." As a result, only one real Puerto Rican was cast, though some auditions were held in East Harlem, and that was Jamie Sanchez, who had acted in legitimate theatre in Puerto Rico before coming to New York more than two years ago. Sanchez won the part of Chino, while Frank Green was signed on as Mouthpiece of the Jets. Green had learned how to use a knife in Texas before improving his technique in the Marines, and this expertise was very useful to Robbins in choreographing the rumble.

Robbins was lucky to find Mickey Calin, a former stuntman. Calin was first told he had no chance, but six months after his initial audition he was called back, only to be informed by his agent that he had failed. However, while touring with *The Boy Friend*, he auditioned again, and then while in stock in Valley Forge, Pennsylvania, he learned that he was cast as Riff.

Things were no easier for Ken Le Roy, brought up in the Bronx and the son of vaudevillians, who was nearly fed up with performing. He had been a winner on *Chance of a Lifetime*, and had done many shows, but he wanted to be a director. He actually came on board the show as an assistant stage manager, but one day, after having watched and heard auditions for many months, he was asked to read for four different roles. These were eventually narrowed to three, and then he was finally picked as Bernardo, leader of the Sharks.

Chita Rivera was easier to find and cast than any of the other principals, for she had appeared in three Broadway shows and had had an interesting training. After studying ballet at eleven with Doris Jones in Washington, D.C., she moved to New York City with her family, where at the age of sixteen she auditioned for George Balanchine and won a scholarship to the School of American Ballet. She took classes in the company of Edward Villella and Melissa Hayden, studying there for three years and then taking jazz dance with Peter

Gennaro and Frank Wagner. She began her professional dance career in 1952 in the chorus of the road company of *Call Me Madam*, appearing under her original name, Dolores Conchita del Rivero. She did a cross-country tour in this musical before returning to New York to replace Onna White as a principal dancer in *Guys and Dolls*. The following year she appeared in *Can-Can*, and although Gwen Verdon won most of the applause for exuberance, Rivera was particularly notable. In 1955 she had her first big hit with *The Shoestring Revue*, a low-budget production that was consistently witty and filled with comic songs. It led to her name-change as Chita Rivera and to appearances on major television shows, as well as in other Broadway shows such as *Seventh Heaven* (1955), a weak, musical version of the Janet Gaynor silent-film classic, and *Mr. Wonderful* (1956), a musical which starred Sammy Davis, Jr.

Rivera's Latin temperament and dance training were perfect for the part of Anita in *West Side Story*, and she phoned a friend, Larry Kert, to urge him to audition. Born Frederick Lawrence Kert in Los Angeles, California, in 1930, he had studied acting with Sanford Meisner at the Neighborhood Playhouse, and singing with Keith Davis, before making his professional début as a member of a group called Bill Norvas and the Upstarts. The group played in cabaret and variety shows, including an engagement at the Roxy in New York. His musical comedy début had come at the Coronet, New York, in 1950, when he appeared in the chorus of *Tickets, Please*. This was a modest success, and not in the same league as *Mr. Wonderful*, which was contemporary in setting and sound. It was in this show that Kert befriended Rivera, because he had a chorus number behind her. That summer he had been the male lead in *Fat Tuesday* at a Catskills resort. It was a show about gang warfare and he performed a number, "No More Mambo," about never going out at night because of fear. Cheryl Crawford, who had not yet pulled out of *West Side Story* at the time, had seen him but not offered much encouragement about a possible audition. It was only after she had dropped the project that Kert heard that the producers wanted to see him for the role of Bernardo. He auditioned, heard a polite "Thank you, very much," and that was that. He heard that he wasn't Puerto Rican enough. A little later, while working on a television show called *Washington Square*, he was called back. Robbins had five others auditioning for Riff, and asked Kert to do "Cool." However, there was too much dancing involved, and Kert, content with chorus-line work, simply did not dance well enough for Riff. As he explained in *Sondheim & Co.*, "Though I had rehearsed at night with Jerry Robbins, unbeknownst to some people, I couldn't make the dancing." By now he had chalked up four weeks of audition time. Then Burt Shevelove called with an offer to do an industrial show he was directing for *Esquire*. Kert performed a calypso, which Stephen Sondheim saw. Afterwards Sondheim asked him to audition for Tony. Kert protested: "But every day you read that Leonard Bernstein is looking for a six-foot, blond, Polish tenor. I'm a five-foot-eleven, dark, Jewish baritone!" But Sondheim encouraged him to audition, and Kert sang "Maria" in the original key, cracking on the high note. Still, the show's creators saw something that they liked and had him do it again one note lower. As Kert was leaving the audition, Ruth Mitchell, the stage manager, introduced him to Carol Lawrence in the lobby. Just then, the Big Four (Laurents, Robbins, Bernstein, Sondheim) passed by and asked them to walk on stage together and sing "Tonight." The song had just been added to the show because "Somewhere" and "One Hand, One Heart" were not, in the opinion of Oscar Hammerstein, enough to make the balcony scene soar. There had been rumours that Anna Maria Alberghetti and Frank Purretta had been original choices for the two leads, but the Big Four were still keeping their options open, even though Kert had failed in all his previous auditions, and Carol Lawrence had already appeared before the casting bosses no less than twelve times.

Lawrence, a year older than Rivera, came from an old-fashioned Italian family in the tiny town of Melrose Park, west of Chicago. It was a loud, oppressive family environment, filled with screaming matches between her parents, but Carolina Maria (her real name) found escape at the Edna McCrae School of Dance, where at the age of twelve she joined professionals in tap class. She began a professional career at thirteen, having changed her name from Carolina Maria Laraia to Carol Laraia and then to Carol Lawrence, because her own father had persuaded her to do so — as she wrote in her autobiography: "People can't read Laraia. So they won't remember it, too many vowels in a row. And if you're going to sing and dance in front of a lot of people, you want them to remember who you are." She performed only on weekends, mostly in local clubs and private halls on Chicago's South Side. Then she went to Northwestern University, but refused to study law (as her father had wanted). She worked in a freshman production, was named "Freshman of the Year in Drama," and was awarded a scholarship. Her obsession with theatre was fanned and she decided to go to New York to learn what it was really like to try out for a show. There she joined a "cattle call" (open audition) for *Borscht Capades*, a kind of Catskills revue. She won a part in the chorus, and worked with Joel Grey and his father, Mickey Katz, who was the star. Also in the cast were Phil Harris and the Barry Sisters. Lawrence didn't get beyond the chorus, but she and another girl spoke the opening lines of the prologue while they were dressed in white ten-gallon hats, short, fringed skirts, and white cowboy boots. Another important break was *New Faces of 1952*, where she worked with Eartha Kitt, Ronny Graham, Alice Ghostley, and Paul Lynde. The revue's success derived from skits and comic lyrics, and the show lasted a year on Broadway before going on the road for another year. At nineteen, Lawrence found herself gainfully employed, always working in some show or other. Summer stock in Highland Park, outside Chicago, taught her to become a quick study, for she did a different show a week — from *Guys and Dolls* to *Oklahoma!* and from *Anything Goes* to *Finian's Rainbow*. The ambitious ingénue took voice and singing lessons from Sue Seton, who later trained Audrey Hepburn, Katharine Hepburn, and Melina Mercouri, and Lawrence's next big opportunity came with an offer of the lead in *Pipe Dream* (1955), a musical by Rodgers and Hammerstein, based on Steinbeck's *Sweet Thursday*. However, a contract as soloist in the opera-season ballets with the Lyric Opera prevented her from accepting the job, but she was to find satisfaction in the chorus of the long-running hit, *Plain and Fancy* (1955), an unpretentious musical that avoided easy theatrical tricks. A bigger role followed in *Shangri-La* (1956), a musicalization of James Hilton's

Lost Horizon, but the show was too cumbersome and had a very short run, although it had Dennis King, Jack Cassidy, Martyn Green, Harold Lang, and Alice Ghostley in its cast. Fortunately for Lawrence, she immediately went into *Ziegfeld Follies* (1957), with Bea Lillie and Billy DeWolfe, which ran about six months despite skimpy production values and recycled material. Within the same period, Lawrence began her determined auditions for *West Side Story*.

Robbins remembers her turning up for the first time, heavily made up and bejewelled in an attempt to look like a Puerto Rican Juliet. "I told her to go home and take a shower and come back." She had numerous call backs, and almost to the end she ran even with a Lebanese girl whose voice was greatly admired. Her thirteenth tryout (which Actors Equity would not permit today) brought her and Larry Kert together. She asked if her partner and she could take the scenes home for memorization and, once Robbins agreed, this is precisely what she and Kert did. "That was a risk," Kert explained to Joan Peyser. "People tend to be more lenient when performers have the music in their hands, but Carol decided to go for broke, and we worked on 'Tonight' for three or four days. At that time it was a twelve-minute scene, there was so much glorious music in it." The pair finally felt comfortable with it, but Robbins devised a surprise. Carol Lawrence remembers that instead of asking the pair to sing a few songs, he instructed Kert to wait backstage. Then, pointing to Lawrence, he said: "You, Maria. See that scaffolding up there over the stage? Look around, find out how to get up there. Then stay there, out of sight." She found a narrow metal ladder and up she went before Robbins called Kert onstage and told him to find Maria and take the scene from there. Up where she was, the actress began to feel as if she were really the character, watching Tony's desperate attempt to find her while afraid to call out to him in case this would alert her family.

Kert was baffled when he entered. He looked around for his Maria but couldn't find her. By the time he saw her and climbed up, the two were almost breathless as they performed the balcony scene. Kert's shimmying up the ladder lent a sense of urgency to the moment and showed some of his physical agility.

At the end, when they descended the ladder, they saw Bernstein walking up to the front of the house. "I don't know what's going to happen," he said. "We have more people we promised to hear. But that is the most mesmerizing audition I have ever seen." Carol Lawrence burst into tears of relief, as Harold Prince comforted her: "No, really — you're Maria!"

That night, Kert was alone at home. At 7:58 Arthur Laurents telephoned: "We've been sitting around and they all said I should break the news to you." That sounded ominous. But he continued: "How does it feel to have a lead on Broadway?" The next morning, Sam Zolotoff ran an item in his newspaper column: "Leonard Bernstein has found his Romeo and Juliet in Larry Kent [sic] and Carol Lawrence." Kert told Joan Peyser: "The first time my name was in the paper, it was misspelled."

Rehearsals began at the Chester Hale Studio which stood on 56th Street near Carnegie Hall. It was really a loft above a garage and small by present-day rehearsal-space standards, but in four weeks Robbins and his cast managed to stage some of the numbers, with the assistance of co-choreographer, Peter Gennaro, who did most of "America," and the Sharks' dances in the dance-hall competition. Robbins wanted eight weeks of rehearsal — unprecedented at the time — because he was a chronic perfectionist who, as Prince remarked in *Contradictions*, "would like the opening-night reviews in his hands" before beginning rehearsal. "He is gun-shy. He hates to go into rehearsal. He's the fellow standing on the edge of a precipice; you, the producer, have to push him over (which naturally makes *you* responsible if the show fails!). But when he finally goes, of course, it's galvanic."

Rehearsals were painful for the cast — as Larry Kert stated years later in several magazine interviews. "Jerry Robbins is an incredible man and I'd work for him in a minute, but he is a painful man — a perfectionist who sees himself in every role, and if you come onstage and don't give him exactly what he's pictured the night before, his tolerance level is too low, so in his own kind of way, he destroys you. People thought we were puppets on strings and in some ways we were."

Robbins was what is commonly called "a Method director" — that is, someone schooled in the Actors Studio system of investigating text as a psychological rather than a literary document. Roles were to be analyzed not simply for simple motivations or goals but for sociological and psychological case histories. *West Side Story* had no chorus. Each gang member was given a name and case history. Most of the actors had had only dance experience in other shows, so Robbins exploited their naiveté. Craig Zadan describes how he forbade them to use their own names, and would always call them in groups, "You're the Jets," and "You're the Sharks." He would bring in articles about interracial street fights and post them on bulletin boards. He made certain by draconian means that the cast members thoroughly identified with their respective gangs. "This stage is the only piece of territory you really own in the theatre," he announced. "Nothing else belongs to you. You've got to fight for it." The actors travelled in packs away from the theatre, and they were encouraged to cut out newspaper accounts of gang rivalries and paste these to the rear walls of the stage. They were also made to eat lunch in their separate groups. This generated so much antagonism that the two male leads, generally best friends, never ate together during the entire rehearsal period. But no one suffered more than Lee Becker, who was playing Anybodys, the cruelly named reject of the Jets. She complained: "No one will eat with me!" and she was forced to take her lunch alone.

The cast learned very quickly that Robbins demanded more of them than they ever thought they could give. They rehearsed and lived by strict rules. To prevent them from slipping out of character, he would suddenly ask them about their characters' parents, even if these parents were not mentioned in the show. Backstage relationships were not to be radically different from onstage role playing. Violence and sexual intimidation, fights and injuries were realities, and Robbins was unmerciful in his pursuit of perfection. "The slightest mistake in a dance step, gesture or word met a fate worse than death," wrote Lawrence in her autobiography. "Almost daily, Jerry would single someone out for criticism — for the entire day! 'You don't know what to do with your hands!' he would shout at that person. 'Keep them in your pockets, damn you!' " Or he would scoff at a player reluctant to pull out all stops: "What do you think that is? You're not reaching hard enough. Make it bigger. You'd think you were wearing a cocktail dress. You make it big. I'll cut it down."

Robbins' harsh methods of directing extended even to his leads. Larry Kert claimed that Robbins seemed to control the whole enterprise. "That's a B-flat, not a G-major chord," he would remark to a singer, or "That skirt is an inch too short." Kert got a lot of trouble from him, so much so that the actor found himself crying much of the time. But Carol Lawrence was a victim as well. She recalls in her autobiography that for the dramatic moment when Tony climbs in through a window after having killed her brother, she was directed to beat her fists against Kert's chest and then drop to the floor. For the longest time Robbins wasn't satisfied that Kert's Tony looked properly guilty about what he had done, so he told Lawrence and Kert to go to the balcony with him where he could work on the scene without holding up the rest of the cast. Then he rehearsed the pair for hours, whispering to Lawrence to hit Kert harder and make him *feel* the guilt and pain. Robbins broke for dinner only after he was satisfied that his Maria had beat Tony's chest with all her might.

Later in her dressing room, Lawrence heard a knock. It was Kert. "He wasn't wearing a shirt, and his entire chest was heavily taped." He had visited a doctor during the dinner break because of severe chest pains. After taping him up, the doctor directed him to caution Lawrence against hitting the actor on the chest again because there was a real danger that his lungs might be loosened from the rib cage. Lawrence sobbed with guilt as Kert wondered aloud, "What'll we do?" The problem was how to tell Robbins.

Lawrence determinedly made her way to the director to announce that she couldn't hit Kert's chest again — at least not in the near future. Without missing a beat, Robbins responded: "Hit him in the head — you can't do any damage there." And it did not sound at all as if he were joking.

Originally, the parts of Maria and Tony called for singing but no dancing. This frustrated Lawrence, especially when she had to watch dance-ins substitute for her and Kert in certain scenes. At the end of each rehearsal, she would say, "Mr. Robbins, I also dance." "Yes, dear," he would reply, as if he had heard that line too many times. Eventually, however, Kert and Lawrence were allowed to learn the big romantic second-act ballet, which enabled the pair to fully experience one of the loveliest moments in the show.

But Lawrence paid for her ambition. As the choreography evolved during rehearsals, the dancing became more athletic and demanding. Robbins kept reminding his cast that they were not people, but the "embodiments" of his creative ideas. He called out orders to them as if they were a military unit. In one scene, where Maria was supposed to be picked up by a group of boys, carried high over their heads, and then cast through the air into the arms of another group, Robbins called out, "Now — the Maria Throwers, pick up Maria, that's right — no, no, put her down and do that again . . . You're too slow . . . The Maria Throwers, pick up Maria . . . *Now*, you Maria Catchers, *catch* her!"

The routine was repeated many times before he was satisfied, but then Robbins ordered one more repetition. Lawrence was picked up and pitched into the air. But Robbins happened to be momentarily distracted and didn't call out for the Catchers to be ready, and the poor Catchers, terrified of him, would not dare make a move unless he gave the command. So Lawrence went crashing to the floor, landing on her stomach and having the wind knocked out of her. All action stopped, as everyone — except Robbins — feared that she might be dead or seriously injured. Lawrence slowly lifted her head to find her "three understudies leaning out from the wings with that terrible look of hopeful anticipation on their faces." That was enough to revive her. "I'm fine, Jerry!" she said quickly. "Well, then, do it again!" he said. "And this time, do it with the Maria Catchers!"

She was in pain for a long time after this accident, but never let Robbins see it. The discipline and dedication she had acquired as a dancer helped her — as well as the realization that Robbins had lived all his life in the ballet world where "the choreographer and dancers played 'master and slaves.'" As she reflected: "It was his modus operandi to berate and belittle us into anger so we would prove him wrong by jumping higher or turning faster or hitting each other harder in a fight sequence. He drove us to fear or hate him — sometimes both. But the result permitted us to experience a potential in ourselves that we would otherwise never have known existed."

Robbins's style was the antithesis of Prince's or Bernstein's. "Jerry's style of putting together a show is different from mine," commented Prince. "In those days I just watched. I wasn't a director yet. I found later that if I'm not liked I can't work. I *hate* turmoil. Jerry Robbins is a man who likes the excitement that comes of contest." For his part, Leonard Bernstein was sensitive to the feelings, needs, and anxieties of the cast. Very often after Robbins had savaged the actors, Bernstein would console them. None of the singers was an opera singer, yet they were all singing opera. But if Bernstein saw that they were having trouble with a passage, he would say, "Tell me, how does that note feel in your mouth? If it doesn't feel comfortable, I'll change it." When Larry Kert asked for help, Bernstein sent him to a retired voice teacher who lived in an uptown hotel. Kert: "It was she and my instincts that got me through the role." Carol Lawrence: "He would work with each of us on an individual basis for hours, and we couldn't take our eyes off his face, because so many emotions were written there. He never lost his temper or his good manners. He didn't drive us; he led us by believing in us."

Bernstein's diary recorded his excitement:

New York; July 8, 1957. Rehearsals. Beautiful sketches for sets by Oliver. Irene showed us costume sketches: breathtaking. I can't believe it: forty kids are actually doing it up there on stage! Forty kids singing five-part counterpoint who never sang before — and sounding like heaven. I guess we were right not to cast "singers": anything that sounded more professional would inevitably sound more experienced, and then the "kid" quality would be gone. A perfect example of a disadvantage turned into a virtue.

Despite the very different personalities and temperaments of the leading collaborators, the production period was one of the most exciting in Broadway history, because all the composers, designers, and crew were mutually supportive. As Robbins remarked in *Broadway Song & Story*: "Arthur would come in with a scene, the others would say they could do a song on this material, I'd supply, 'How about if we did this as a dance?' . . . the essence of it was what we gave to each other, took from each other, yielded to each other, surrendered, reworked, put back together again, all of those things."

The strengths of the show, for Laurents, were the Romeo and Juliet story and the contemporary application. Shakespeare had had more time and space to tell his story, but Laurents thought that the topicality of the main situations gave his libretto a genuine force. Like Romeo, Tony was "a callow lovesick boy," although, unfortunately, both were the worst-drawn characters in their respective stories. The main trouble was to create a story without too much socioeconomic background. In *Sondheim & Co.* Laurents explains: "You get a very quick abortive scene with the two boys and another little scene to introduce the girl. When I originally wrote the book I didn't have those introductory scenes but Jerry wanted them and he was right."

Laurents made up his own slang, because he knew that if he used real contemporary slang, it would date too quickly. "But even the Puerto Rican talk, saying *kiddando* instead of *kid*, was all made up. It sounded very jivey. They never used *cool* then — that word came into the language much later. I twisted syllables and did all sorts of things because the show needed a language. It was lyric theater and if you used actual language it would have been flat."

"Arthur had the hardest job of anybody converting a Shakespeare play into musical theater of today," acknowledged Jerome Robbins in *Broadway Song & Story*. "Lenny, Steve and I had nothing to put our work against. Arthur had the text by Mr. William S all the time. We could make our poetry out of the music, the dancing, the song lyrics, but Arthur had the burden of making his text go along with *Romeo and Juliet* and still communicate some of the poetry, the argot, the drives and passions of the 1950s, while trying to match, somehow, the style we were creating as we went along."

Although one of the shortest books in Broadway-musical history,

West Side Story is packed with action. The plot is exciting and its leanness impressive, especially as much of the story is communicated without dialogue. This points to the collaborative nature of the project. For instance, the prologue originally had words. The extraordinary instrumental music was first sung. Bernstein: "It didn't take us long to find out that wouldn't work. That was when Jerry took over and converted all that stuff into this remarkable thing now known as 'the prologue to *West Side Story*,' all dancing and movement."

Originally, too, the production had an opening number (after the prologue) called "Mix." This was an exciting song, but as Bernstein acknowledged in *Notes on Broadway*, "you couldn't understand anything the players were saying because it was too fast, too complicated, too canonical, too contrapuntal. So we wrote another one, called 'The Jet Song.' "

Bernstein's hectic, feverish music caught the mood of restless, hostile, slum youth so well that it certainly paid off its composer's research. Bernstein and Robbins had both gone to various locales in Brooklyn Heights and old areas of encrusted gentility now going through great changes.

In the course of their attempts to know the social reality of the play, Robbins lurked around the dark streets of the Barrio, the fringes of the Village, and the "jungle" of the Red Hook, recognizing how insulated he and his partners were. He said to David Boroff: "My office is on Lexington Avenue and 74th Street and just twenty blocks away life is entirely different. The streets are darker, the signs are in Spanish, and the people lead their lives on the sidewalks. Those kids live like pressure cookers. There's a constant tension, a feeling of the kids having steam that they don't know how to let off."

Robbins actually witnessed the beginning of a rumble between two gangs at an Italian fiesta in downtown Manhattan. As he reported to John Keating of *Cue*: "It was frightening. You could feel the tension so thick . . . I don't actually know why the whole thing didn't erupt. Later on, I sneaked up behind a knot of the kids and listened to them calmly discussing whether they could settle whatever the argument was by a fair fight." One of his most informative experiences in this research was a Brooklyn dance, where one gang was formally decked out in red plaid ties, red plaid cummerbunds, plain red shirts and socks, and another gang in short black coats with velvet collars, cuffs, and pocket flaps. As for the dancing, Robbins was amazed: "Everyone danced by himself — it was a floor full of soloists. Later, after watching a bit, you discovered that they started with a partner, but after four bars or so, everyone took off on his own. But, make no mistake — everyone knew what his partner was doing at any given moment. There was no cutting in." On the slow numbers, it was the opposite, for the couples were "pasted together and almost immediately went into a grind routine. But the boys played it real cool: they would try to anticipate the end of the number and would break and just walk off the floor a moment before the end." What impressed him the most, as he recounted to Keating, was "the sense they gave you of containing their own world. Not arrogance, exactly; but a crazy kind of confidence. And there was always a sense of tension. At dances, you got the impression they were trying to exorcise their own tensions."

All this fed, of course, into his staging of the dance in the gym. The dance challenges were forms of competitive sex and violence, all expressed in a wonderful series of movement and dance phrases. Robbins explained to David Boroff that the slum youth lived in one of the "worst worlds possible" and so they felt that they had to live their lives passionately and without delay. There had recently been a stabbing at Orchard Beach, arising from a dispute about possession of a beach area. "Why does a gang have to own Bay 13? Just the fact that at home they have to band together to 'own' a piece of terrible block. Yet they have a fantastic sense of security when they are together. . . . They want love, but only the gang is their family." Obviously, this insight informed his method of keeping his actors in character throughout rehearsals and into the Broadway run of the show.

There was an artistic symbiosis between Robbins and cast — particularly the dancers. It was clear to everybody in the production that he was trying to make the characters as real as possible, although the show itself was not a documentary. His dance ensemble consisted of sixteen males and eight females. The preponderance of boys was on account of gang membership, and each dancer had a name and identity. One day every member of the Sharks came to rehearsal with a strip of wool around his wrist as a gang insignia. Robbins would interpret the play for them and help them find an emotional basis for the movements. "I want my dancers, just as in acting, to find an emotional justification for an extension or whatever movement they're doing," he explained in *Dance Magazine*. "I want them to understand who they are and what they are." His dancers, in turn, helped shape some of his ideas: "I am influenced by the dancers. I see how they move, and this stimulates my own creative thinking."

But so much seriousness had a price. At the first run-through, about three weeks into rehearsal, the show seemed (in Harold Prince's words) "slow, lugubrious, somewhat self-conscious, IMPORTANT. Too much introspection, no impulse, no energy. Fear struck." It was now evident to Prince that Robbins had been far too obsessed with Actors Studio exercises in improvisation, sense memory, and private moments, and what the show really needed were "old-fashioned line readings," without pregnant pauses and weighty, measured phrasings. After some discussion with Laurents, Robbins was persuaded to discard the Method, and the company "snapped to so quickly that at the next run-through, less than a week later, the show was in good shape." And yet, there was no denying that all the preliminary discussion, improvisation, and exploration of the spines of the characters had helped give the show a strong foundation.

Inevitably, the collaborators' efforts overlapped. Laurents took a lot, of course, from Shakespeare. Robbins often choreographed with Bernstein close by. In *Broadway Song & Story*, Bernstein reminisced: "I remember all my collaborations with Jerry in terms of one tactile bodily feeling: his hands on my shoulders — composing with his hands on my shoulders. This may be metaphorical, but it's the way I remember it. I can feel him standing behind me saying, 'Four more beats there,' or 'No, that's too many,' or 'Yeah — that's it!'" Or Robbins would suddenly have an inspiration after Bernstein had played something. Bernstein (in his own exaggerated language) "raped" Laurents' book, often using it as a starting point for a lyric.

Sondheim and Bernstein worked together in various ways, but usually in a dimly lit room where vigorous theorizing about what they were writing would often lead to long periods of silence and sometimes sleep. Like Sondheim, Bernstein revelled in games, and the two would play anagrams for hours, interrupted by Bernstein's lethargic attempts to make coffee in a new espresso machine. This informal, relaxed mood did help creativity. The pair worked sometimes as a duo, sometimes separately, sometimes with the tune first ("Cool" and "Gee, Officer Krupke"), sometimes with the words first ("A Boy Like That"). Sondheim admitted to having written one "dry lyric": one evening he got the notion for "A Boy Like That," wrote it out according to a rhythm in his head, and handed it to Bernstein, who set it entirely differently, according to his own rhythm. In a couple of instances, Bernstein actually handed him some discarded music from *Candide*: thus, "Officer Krupke" and "One Hand, One Heart" were both set to tunes from that show, with "Krupke" set to "Where Does It Get You in the End," and "One Hand" to a melody entitled simply "One." Laurents gave his composer and lyricist titles of songs and even lists of what they should be about. But often, the librettist's dialogue supplied the inspiration. Bernstein recalls that " 'Something's Coming' was born right out of a long speech that Arthur wrote for Tony. It said how every morning he would wake up and reach out for something, around the corner or down the beach."

Late in rehearsals, Bernstein and Sondheim realized that Tony needed a strong song earlier in the play than "Maria." They wanted more delineation of him as a character. They were looking at a particular speech in the script when "Something's Coming" just seemed to leap off the page. In the course of the day they had composed the song. Something similar happened when Sondheim pounced on a very prosaic line in the libretto and turned it into "A Boy Like That." Only very rarely did they work against the text. The most striking instance was for the finale. Craig Zadan quotes Laurents: "One of the funny things is that I meant for the girl to sing again at the very end when she picks up the gun. The dialogue I wrote was meant as a rough outline for a dummy lyric for what she should sing. And that's what she says to this day — they just never wrote the song, they decided that there shouldn't be one."

Robbins played a crucial role, too, in the development of words and music. In *Broadway Song & Story*, Sondheim relates that when Robbins heard "Maria" for the first time, he asked boldly: "Now what happens there?" Sondheim replied: "Well, you know, he is standing outside her house and, you know, he senses that she's going to appear on the balcony." "Yeah, but what is he doing?" "Oh, he's standing there and singing a song." Robbins asked: "*What is he doing?*" Sondheim could only offer rather lamely: "Well, he sings, 'Maria, Maria, I just met a girl named Maria and suddenly that name will never be the same to me.' " Robbins persisted: "And then what happens?" "Then he sings . . ." "You mean," Robbins asked incredulously, "he just stands looking at the audience?" "Well, yes." "*You* stage it," Robbins said disgustedly.

Sondheim saw through the director's grumpiness to the fundamental point. After all, "Maria" was not an art song; nor was it simply presentational — something an actor could just go out and sing. It was part of a dramatic action, meant to carry the story forward in some way, and Robbins was asking for something to play so that the audience would be interested. As he remarks in *Broadway Story & Song*, this is when Sondheim realized that composing a song was like plotting or choreographing in your head: "We [songwriters] should be able to tell the director and the choreographer, 'All right, now when he starts to sing the song he's sitting down in a chair. Now around the second quatrain he gets up and crosses to the fireplace and throws her note in the fireplace. Then he sings the third quatrain directly to the audience, then he goes back and shoots himself and sings the fourth quatrain.'"

Apart from the one sticky business about "Maria" and Robbins' initial insecurity about his own ballets — where he asked for a special song to be delivered in a disembodied voice explaining to the audience what the ballets were about — the production developed without any of the collaborators feeling anything less than vital to the overall success of the show.

From Tryout to Opening

THERE WERE FEW CHANGES during the tryout period. Robbins felt strongly that the middle of the first act sagged, so the composers wrote "Kids Ain't" for Anybodys, A-rab, and Baby John. This was a terrific trio that almost everybody loved, but Laurents delivered an eloquent argument against it because it was too much of a crowd-pleaser and would tip the show into typical musical comedy. So it never went in. Then there was a new opening because Robbins did not feel that the original was violent enough. However, the new one ("This Turf Is Ours") was deemed *too* violent, so it was scrapped and the show returned to "Jet Song," which was given a new release.

In Washington, Robbins wanted a special sound for the second-act ballet — something "almost rhythmless, as though from a string quartet." At the technical rehearsal, he went to the front row, leaned over Max Goberman who was conducting and instructed him to circle each of the notes to be deleted. Upon observing this, Bernstein arose from his auditorium seat and disappeared. Sondheim later found him in a bar with three scotches lined up before him.

But despite Robbins' alterations, the show preserved its unique integration of movement, dance, song, and text. Not that all was sweetness and light in Washington. The weather that August was uncomfortably hot, and nobody knew whether audiences would really listen to the show or even stay inside the theatre. On opening night, there was a telephone message for the producers from *La Prensa* that threatened a picket if the show travelled to New York without cutting or altering the song "America." The objection was to the phrase "island of tropical diseases," because the reference was taken as an insult not only to Puerto Rico but its people as well.

However, the producers did nothing about the threat, and the show was not picketed.

The opening won strong applause. At the intermission, Supreme Court Justice Felix Frankfurter met Bernstein in the lobby and remarked, "The history of America is now changed." Richard Coe of *The Washington Post* called *West Side Story* a "work of art," and a "romance of the lonely for the lonesome." Extolling the "immensely appealing" performances of Rivera and Lawrence, he also remarked on the "tremendously alert performances" by Calin, Kert, and Le Roy, and devoted the major part of his praise to Bernstein's "flowing music that jells the vitality of these young people at their pitiably innocent warfare." However, Coe failed to mention the name of Sondheim, and the lyricist was understandably upset: "I ended up writing all the lyrics and received no mention in Washington. I was really unhappy. Bernstein knew it and came to me and generously offered to take his name off the lyric credit and even give me the concomitant royalty fee." Bernstein also called Sondheim's agent, Flora Roberts, to say that he would contact the music publisher and his own agent to reprint the music with only Sondheim's name listed as lyricist. This entailed a fair amount of work and money, because the first signature (or batch of pages) had to be reprinted for the inside titles as well. Some scores had already been completed and bound, so the alteration really involved the title page, the cover, and a rerun of the first signature. Flora Roberts was impressed by Bernstein's generosity, as she told Craig Zadan: "I think, quite frankly, what Lenny did is fairly unheard of in the theater. Too many people get credit for things they don't do, much less remove their names."

In Philadelphia, the next tryout centre, new posters exhibited Sondheim's proper credit, but, alas, the show itself did not receive a reception as favourable as in Washington — though there was praise from Henry Murdock in the *Inquirer* ("a grown-up musical"), Wayne Robinson in the *Bulletin* ("an exciting evening"), and Jerry Gaghan in the *News* ("topical and shocking"). At a special run-through for Oscar Hammerstein, Sondheim was informed by his mentor that "Tonight" did not soar sufficiently for the balcony scene. "It's a nice song," said Hammerstein, "but it doesn't seem to me to take off enough." Sondheim trusted his friend's instinct, and he also knew that "the truth was that the song had not been written for that scene but was used there as a last resort." But the song remained intact, as did "I Feel Pretty," which another friend, Sheldon Harnick, criticized for being inappropriate to Maria's character in diction and rhyme. "Sheldon was very gentle, but oh! did it hurt." As Sondheim well realized: "Well, when rhyme goes against character, out it should go, and rhyme always implies education and mind working, and the more rhymes the sharper the mind." Sondheim tried a simplified version of the lyric so that his Puerto Rican heroine would not sound like someone welcomed in Noël Coward's living room, but nobody connected with the show wanted it, and his original lines remained to embarrass him every time they were sung.

The show received only mild praise, but the collaborators remained calm. "Philly is an anti theatrical town," Sondheim would eventually comment. "Later, when *Gypsy* opened in Philly, I met Mike Nichols, who told me that it was the only city in the world that he and Elaine May would never play again . . . that they'd played hamlets in the Deep South rather than Philly."

Regardless of the sour critics, the box office thrived. Bernstein was rapturous, for as he wrote in a letter to David Diamond, a fellow composer: "It really does my heart good — because this show is my baby, my tragic musical-comedy, whatever that is; and if it goes in New York as it has on the road, we will have proved something very big indeed, and maybe changed the face of the American musical theater."

Bernstein did not have long to wait for the New York reception. The show opened on September 26, 1957, at the Winter Garden Theatre.

⋆　⋆　⋆

The curtain rose on a silence — or was it, perhaps, simply a pause? — what Walter Kerr would call in his *Herald Tribune* review "the last silence and the last pause." No overture — that would be for the film later — simply Oliver Smith's scenic décor that could have been lifted from a rotting tenement in the Bronx, where inhabitants lived four or six to a room and paid for the privilege of sharing their miserable existence with rats and cockroaches. But the audience was not inside any such tenement; it was, instead, in a midsummer cityscape of warehouses that were harsh, gloomy, and barren under a lazy, overcast sky (created by Jean Rosenthal). And against this wasteland of broken windows, peeling plaster, and crumbling walls there was a group of blue-jacketed young delinquents, with their tribal name "Jets" scrawled high across their taut backs. They were lounging — but not simply lounging. Their bodies had a faint stirring of impatience. And then that stirring became the first sounds of the play — a finger snapping, accompanied by knee movements.

Suddenly another gang appeared — equally young, more homogeneous in look and colour, but sharing with the Jets old hatreds whose original cause nobody recalled. These had their own costume colours and facial tan, and they poured out from alleyways. The brief silence had edged into sounds of incipient mayhem. A sneer, a hiss, gestures of contempt or intimidation exchanged and flicked back and forth with wrists and thrusting arms. This was a ritualized war — the site itself being the booty. And with each body movement, every gesture, or the merest signal of threat and retaliation, the ritual grew more elaborate, the tension more choreographed. And then a powerful downbeat of Max Goberman's orchestra, and the ritual reached a frenzy as youths were grabbed, pummelled, chased off, blocked, always with the essential pattern of two advancing groups determined to bare teeth and clench fists in a multiplication of fresh excitement. The jazz rhythms raced, with pulsing, throbbing chords building tension.

The audience was observing a raw life force, at first guarded in its slow seething but all too quickly bursting out of an ominous pause. And the actors' bodies dramatized the emotion even before the first eruption of music. The gangs reached an ecstasy of delinquency in concert with the brutal music, and even as the walls of the rotting city pressed in on their coiled bodies, bodies first stealthy and then openly insolent, the youths used their own violence as a symbol of tension.

Once the fight had been interrupted by a police whistle and the arrival of Schrank and Krupke, there were strips of dialogue which laid out the crude sociology of the story in the distinctive diction and idioms of Arthur Laurents. This was not high literature, to be sure, and it was as far from Shakespeare (even at his most prosaic) as the earth from the sun, but the shrill, metallic music of the prologue and the *graceful* violence of the gangs had already prepared the audience for some of the stridencies in the dialogue. Within a very few minutes of the opening, there was a new sound, texture, and look for a Broadway musical.

The first scene reached a climax in the "Jet Song," a defiant anthem of gang brotherhood that built with wry humour mixed into the demotic diction of asphalt hoodlums. Gestures of denigration and intimidation became an exultation, and what the song's lyric projected about a conquest of territory was a prelude to Robbins' conquest of space by dance. As yet, venom was only theatrical: there had been a boiling over of tempers, but no visible blood. And the song converted primitivism into a joyous game. The prologue had grown out of the first silent contraction of a few bodies on an empty stage, then had reached a frenzy of expansion through movement. The story then contracted into an expository scene, only to expand again into a sparkling choral number, where the demonic pulse of the story beat and where the rushed, driving pulse had a restless energy.

The Romeo of the piece came on plainly, but his mood and character soon developed in his first song, "Something's Coming." Larry Kert looked young, fresh, simple — a juvenile with a vague excitement. Oliver Smith had put this urban Romeo against a background of loads of wash hung out to dry. And the lyric sought to find a poetry adequate to this Romeo's spirit. Though it failed to match image or diction to emotion, the verse structure and musical rhythm expanded Tony's yearning in elongated assonances and rhymes, so that with the blackout the falling cadence never really ended.

Carol Lawrence and Chita Rivera were the first real feminine notes in the show, as they appeared together in a bridal shop where Maria, newly arrived in the U.S., was bemoaning the strict restrictions placed upon her by her brother. Lawrence brought a sweet maidenliness to her role in contrast to the flashing fire of Rivera who, instead of being the equivalent of Shakespeare's playful Nurse, was a whirlwind and a colourful foil. The end of their spirited discussion of Maria's new life in America and her lack of interest in Chino, her suitor, led directly into one of Oliver Smith's stunningly colourful scene-changes. As Lawrence whirled in her white communion dress, the shop slid off and a flood of coloured streamers (lavender, pink, green) poured down, accompanied by entrances of the two gangs. Irene Sharaff's dungareed delinquents were all dressed up now: the Jets were in ochres and blues, with velvet pockets, collars, and cuffs; the Sharks were in reds, violets, pinks, and black.

Now came one of the most exciting moments in the play — the "Dance at the Gym" — where the hot colours of the streamers and lights and the hot music — jive, then mambo — increased the visual delights and maintained the same pattern of contraction and expansion already experienced in the prologue. This was not just an exhilarating set piece of show-stopping verve, but a carnival contest where choreography expressed emotion and where plot was actually catalyzed by the rival styles of dance, resulting in a flare-up.

The Jets' jive was countered by the Sharks' quick, quick, slow, slow rhythm. Mickey Calin's Riff looked like Elvis Presley, and although he did not indulge in hip gyrations or pelvic thrusts, he made the gym hop with his bounce and drive. Ken Le Roy's Bernardo and Chita Rivera's Anita were more than eager to compete on the dance floor. Their attack and sensuousness had a palpable carnal edge. Both jive and mambo allowed for variation in steps, though the mambo offered a greater scope, especially as it could be executed in open or closed positions, with the partners either apart from or in close contact with one another. With knees flexed at all times, with most of the body movement concentrated in the hips, and with neat follow-throughs, the mambo dancers were a spectacular delight, especially with their rapid crossovers and pivots. The multicoloured ruffled skirts of the girls billowed up and out, and the dancers flung their hands straight up over their heads. The audience appreciated the flair and the swirling, stomping challenge to the Jets. With hardly a suspension of momentum, the challenge was accepted — the only pause being the elegant ritual of dancers stepping onto the floor and signalling for their partners. Mickey Calin's virtuoso aerial somersaults and Ken Le Roy's whipping leaps — with a few *glissando* variations and high lifts for Rivera — brought waves of applause, and the magic modulated into a delicate cha-cha as Kert and Lawrence discovered each other after the jazz and Latin wildness of music and dance.

As they walked slowly to each other, dancers scattered (although some still danced slowly in the background) and the lights changed for this first rapture. Raising arms to shoulder length, they executed a delicate, slow, side step with the lead leg crossed behind. A slow swaying from their flexed knees created a formal symmetry, as the two received impulses from each other. This was a theme-and-variation dance, with the duo in the foreground and the corps in the background, but the focus was always on Tony and Maria in their romantic pavane. This dance had the sort of tenderness hitherto unsuspected in the show, and by their intense concentration, each to each, Tony and Maria created the exquisite loneliness that young lovers must bear as they find heaven in each other's eyes.

As Joseph Swain puts it, Bernstein had built his tragic idiom "into the higher structural levels of *West Side Story*" with the use of two techniques which, "although not new to Broadway, [were] in this play exploited as never before: the continuity of several musical numbers in succession, and the drama of dance." In this section of the musical, "numbers follow[ed] in succession without appreciable break for dialogue," beginning with the mambo, continuing through the cha-cha into "Maria," and ending with the Balcony Scene. There were snippets of dialogue, but music played under all of them, and "various musical connections [left] no doubt that continuity [was] intended."

The effect of Robbins' staging was to portray how Tony and Maria's love arose from a battleground. The mambo itself had been a show of force, and as the lovers caught sight of each other, the lights dimmed and the music began a sequence of progressions.

Shakespeare used the sonnet form to establish a love relationship between his Romeo and Juliet at the Capulet ball. This play, however, developed the relationship compactly and almost wordlessly. The verbal economy was by itself an indication of the lovers' helplessness, and the score was a clever device to make the moment stand out and apart from everything else. The pavane existed, as it were, in a separate world — a point reinforced by the fading light and Maria's soft costume colour. The composer's sensitivity to the romance was shown in the diminution of sound and the use of pizzicato (plucking of strings) and finger snapping in a mild, stylized tango for the "Maria" motif.

"Maria" was Tony's hymn of love, a wonderful release of sentiment with what Swain has called "an astonishing number of wonderful features for its short length." Beginning with Tony's "dazed amazement," the song had an accelerating rhythm, with a rhapsodic, singing counterpoint to the main orchestral tune. The echoing word was Maria's name, as if "Tony's happiness is so boundless that he can do nothing but name its cause."

With "Maria" as the last word in the audience's ears, the lyrical romanticism flowed on into a balcony scene, where a red fire escape hung spidery against a brick wall. As the lovers sang "Tonight," with Larry Kert hugging Lawrence throughout the number, the deep night sky glowed through the brick, and stars peeped out of the firmament. The tonal poetry was strong enough to transcend some of the banalities of brief dialogue, for the lovers had somehow slipped away from a dingy space into free and open heights. Once again, lighting and positioning emphasized their isolation; once again, they were contained in their own private world from which earthly contingencies had slipped momentarily away.

And then there was an abrupt snap back to the sour realism of the present, with fiery Anita sarcastically shaping "America" into a mocking satire. The strident whistling, shouting, clapping, and foot stamping to a marimba beat were a full-blooded return to a society contaminated by vices that Tony and Maria were struggling to evade. "America" was a number of mockery, opprobrium, and defiance. The Puerto Ricans showed off what the country had allowed them to become — freer in body language and emotional display. The young men and women had their respective dance phrases, all marked by surging impulses of energy, which flowed and grew into a drama of contradistinctions. The women's hand clapping competed against the men's fast swirls, the high kicks of the one pulsed against the back kicks and semi-entrechats of the other. The repetitions were never tedious, effecting a finale of diagonals and crossovers, with space between the dancers widening or narrowing, expanding or contracting, in ever-altering configurations.

From here the story accelerated, building in lines of various thicknesses to the great blood-curdling and blood-spattered climax of the first act. In quick succession came the Jets' "Cool" number, the challenge to a rumble, Tony and Maria's enactment of marriage, "Tonight" (Quintet and Chorus), and the double deaths of Riff and Bernardo, so that there was little or no time to sort out the elements that coalesced into a musical romance with tragic undertones.

"Cool" (in the key of C minor) was constructed by a sparse movement of shoulder, hip, or head. A chorus of snaps cued a rocking, swinging ensemble in windbreakers, T-shirts, and jeans. There was bounce in every crouch, a mixture of jazz styles even in the quick, collapsing movements — bent knees and lowered centres of gravity, kicks with out-flung arms, signature poses with variant lines, changes in focus from low to high to low. The choreography was sharp and explosive, yet the dancers' faces remained insolent or indifferent. This dance was a mask — but it never looked superficial or "square." Some steps repeated movements from the prologue, but the dance was not twitch-and-slink or writhe-and-gyrate. There was a fresh excitement generated by the tension of a gang's attempt to control its instinctive drive to mayhem.

And then came another continuous musical sequence, encompassing the bridal shop "marriage," the polytonal "Tonight," and the mad violence of the choreographed rumble. The moving music of "One Hand, One Heart" yielded to the jarring opening of "Tonight," with important musical elements which first appeared in the prologue now returning in their harshest, most dissonant forms. The five principal characters — Tony, Maria, Anita, Bernardo, and

Riff — formed a dramatic quintet in fateful anticipation of the coming evening. Each principal (except Maria) had a solo in the first half, and then there was an intensifying counterpoint on two musical themes. Ironically, the Jets and Sharks sang the same music, while the lovers reprised the words and music from their Balcony Scene. Violence and sublimity mixed together in a musical summary of the symbols and progress of tragedy. Jerome Robbins' staging of this ensemble piece was a special highlight. Maria stood on the fire escape, with figures shadowed below her. Anita was in a diagonal from them, and the two gangs were silhouetted toward the left like (in Harriet Johnson's words) "a couple of 'art constructions' competing with each other." Jean Rosenthal's lighting built with the music to the climax, and the final exultant note ended with a blackout.

The quintet drew prolonged applause, but the sequence flowed on — into the highway at nightfall, where the almost-silhouetted gangs entered from separate sides, climbing over wire fences or crawling through holes in the walls, like animals plotting an attack. Oliver Smith's design created the atmosphere before any action ensued, and drew another wave of applause. The stage was heated by the strained outflung arms, the menacing fingers, the stealthy feet, the pools of venom collecting within these hoodlums. There was a violet colour to the violence, as steel blades glinted. The killing of Mickey Calin's Riff was frozen in a split-second tableau at the point of Ken Le Roy's knife. The ensuing free-for-all was, perhaps, too much of a dance, with kicks and body tackles, thrustings and parryings, all meticulously performed in an escalating rhythm. And yet the rumble was carried to a savage, chilling close as the geyser force of the first act subsided in the faces of a spellbound audience.

The crack of applause and spontaneous cheers were unsurprising. The audience sensed that the show was like newspaper headlines brought garishly to life. But, more than this, *West Side Story* was startling in its form, with arias, duets, choral numbers, ballet and jive, mambo, cha-cha, and a libretto that was taut and lean and sinister. Expectations for the second half were high, although there were questions forming in several critics' minds about a deficiency of the spoken word and the limited warmth in the acting.

The second half opened on what many in the audience felt was an incongruous note. Maria's bedroom contracted space, although Carol Lawrence rhapsodized about feeling "pretty, and witty and bright." Her emotion expanded, pushing the scene into an airiness quite apart from the tragic scheme, and offering comic relief that was rather out of the character's true compass. The song instantly gave the sense of being a hit single, if judged wholly on its own terms and totally removed from the play's context, but Sondheim's lyric made Maria sound too much like a dainty Julie Andrews, though this distraction (aided and abetted by the click of tambourines and cas-tanets) quickly ended with the urgings of the plot — Chino's dra-matic entrance to report on the upcoming rumble. Now Maria and her lover would never have quite the same self-containment in any special dream of their own. They were, it was sharply felt, at the mercy of forces beyond their control, and they were transformed themselves. Lawrence's Maria grew desperately enraged, desper-ately limp in her lover's arms. Words and emotion tumbled out for the first time between these two. Gone was the delicate grace, the haunting tenderness of their first meeting. Gone was the romantic ardour of their balcony bliss. Chaos had come now, battering at their minds and spirits, ripping into places of the heart. True, the actors lacked subtlety, but they were constrained by the arbitrary demands of the script. Luckily, they had another song, "Somewhere," their wish-fulfillment fantasy, which had an extended melodic line. It was a phantasmagoric sequence that suddenly burst briefly into sunlight and "buttermilk" clouds in the open air. With Reri Grist's Consuelo singing in a torn, broken voice off-stage, "Hold my hand and I'm halfway there — I'll take you there — somewhere," the lyric expressed the heartbreaking fact that a spell had broken. As a melody, "Some-where" was quite enough to include within itself echoes of a motif heard in their bridal-shop vows, quite enough to revive echoes of the glinting knife-fights and deaths, and certainly enough, with the aid of Jean Rosenthal's shadowy lighting and Oliver Smith's evaporating and reappearing tenement world, to presage doom in the sinister cello notes, and the sharp, savage, nightmare chords with which the scene shuddered to a fade-out as the lovers sank back on a bed.

The comic relief of "Gee, Officer Krupke" seemed like a satirical violation of solemnity and grave rigidity, for the taunts and comic-strip language had more going for them than the footwork, but this taunting anticipated other moments in the rising action. There was, of course, Anita's disillusioned and bristlingly bitter animosity in "A Boy Like That" — parried and then repulsed by Maria's reply — and both Rivera and Lawrence got full value from the tone clusters, tritones, and dissonances, building with the song to a tremendous moment of closure wherein Anita capitulated to Maria's impressive conviction.

After the fireworks of this song, the plot rushed, raw and jagged, to a midnight catastrophe and redemption. And there was more taunting. The drugstore episode — where Rivera suffered vile abuse and manhandling by the Jets — ensured that the rest of the plot would be, for the most part, dark and ugly. And there was still more provocation — this one in Tony's murderous rage when he cried out for Chino to come and get him. It was a savage challenge, but where the drugstore incident had been an uglier one, this time the sense of devastation was much too palpable to allow for diversions. A figure stepped out of the dark and there was a gunshot. The final violence had a stark brevity.

Finally, the frayed dream would end. Nothing that Lawrence's Maria could say or sing could urge her dying lover to life or to that ideal refuge they had so desperately wanted. The scene worked towards closure through a "Finale" that completed the lovers' story and resolved the gang warfare. "Somewhere" was reprised, with Lawrence singing the end of the song, picking it up where Tony had once done at the end of the nightmare sequence. The orchestra fell silent, for it was strictly her moment to sound the key note and central pitch of the musical.

The play ended on a longer silence than that which had begun it. The finale resolved itself into moving acts whereby Maria threatened to use a gun first against Chino, then against Action, before breaking into tears, hurling the weapon away, and sinking to the ground like a grieving madonna.

The music came up from under the solemn spectacle, and the final image was of a funeral procession conducted by both gangs in concert, witnessed forlornly by the adults, Doc, Schrank, Krupke, and Glad Hand.

Some of the audience sat open-mouthed and gasping at the end. The pieces all fit together, although the hoodlums were insufficiently explained and the acting, although competent, was rushed and did not fill the tragic spaces. Yet as the evening had raced to its conclusion, there had been terror, raw drive, cruel bewilderment, and loss. This was a show that had danced practically all night, to a music that had a jangled power, a macabre insistence, a cool insolence, a blues sadness, and a sometimes soaring beauty.

★ ★ ★

West Side Story did not receive unanimous or even overwhelming approval from Broadway critics, but there were positive remarks from Frank Aston of the *New York World-Telegram and the Sun*, Richard Watts, Jr. of the *New York Post*, John Chapman of the *Daily News*, John McClain of the *Journal American*, and Robert Coleman of the *Daily Mirror*. Aston deemed the show "an eye-popping, ear-soothing, conscience-busting combination" that "moved swiftly from scene to scene, from mood to mood." Watts called it "a somber tragedy" where choreography fused with the story "so effectively that the ugliness and horror of the war to the death between the boys is never lost." As for Bernstein's music, Watts found it vigorous, vital, and harsh. John Chapman felt that the American theatre had taken "a venturesome forward step," and judged that the cast, next to the music, was "the best part of the production." "It is the most exciting thing that has come to town since *My Fair Lady*," crowed John McClain, while Robert Coleman called it "a superlative musical" — "a chiller, a thriller, as up-to-the-minute as tomorrow's headlines."

But even the applauders stirred some controversy. Aston, for example, although quite correct in describing the work as "a marvel peculiar to this country," did not help matters by asserting that "It's fun to have delinquents sing and act their notion of how idiotic they consider juvenile court judges, psychiatrists and social workers." In equating the special nature of the show with a sort of anarchistic frivolity, Aston was radically reducing the seriousness of Laurents' libretto and Bernstein's score. And his colleague, John Chapman, went one misstep farther by describing West Side Story as "a bold new kind of musical theatre — a juke-box Manhattan opera." This should have been cause enough for Bernstein to wince and blush, because Chapman unwittingly lent substance to Serge Koussevitzky's dismissive scorn for Broadway musicals. A juke-box entertainment was hardly Bernstein's mission or achievement, and by breezily equating the show with such capricious populism, Chapman merely made it more difficult for the show's creators to get audiences and critics to take their production with the seriousness appropriate to a work of art. As it was, West Side Story was greeted with some reservations by Wolcott Gibbs, Walter Kerr, Brooks Atkinson, Henry Hewes, and Howard Taubman, and so it did not need any misjudged support.

In general, the dissenters fashioned arguments against both the material and the form. Atkinson thought the "workmanship" admirable, but the material "horrifying." He deplored the "hideousness" of the gang warfare and the facile, forbidding quality of the early scenes. Writing in the New Yorker, Gibbs warned that the show would not bring "much comfort to those who still visit musicals in the wistful hope of seeing valour overcome a certain number of obstacles to capture beauty in the end." Other critics objected for technical reasons. For Henry Hewes in Saturday Review, Bernstein's music seemed nervous and tired, and Sondheim's lyrics only occasionally more than adequate. Kerr complained in the Herald Tribune that the show was not generally well sung and that it was "rushingly acted." He wrote: "The dramatic postures are rarely varied, and it is, apart from the spine-tingling velocity of the dances, almost never emotionally affecting." Then he offered an interesting explanation: ". . . the people often seem to be behaving as they do because of arbitrary commands from a borrowed plot. Perhaps the near-absence of comedy whittles away the substance of ordinary humanity. Perhaps these teen-age gangsters are too ferocious, too tawdry, too intent upon grinding their teeth to interest us compassionately for two and one-half hours."

Kerr's review soured the opening-night party hosted by burly, balding Roger Stevens at Park Avenue's Ambassador Hotel. Cast members sipped champagne and danced to music from *My Fair Lady*, as Robbins wandered in a happy daze, and Bernstein, his greying hair rumpled, appeared in a navy-blue coat draped like a cape over his shoulders. Despite this jaunty touch, he was upset as he waved Kerr's review in front of the guests and remarked that Kerr was "such an inverted snob, such an intellectual, that he cannot stand a musical unless it has a chorus line." There was some truth in his remark, for Kerr had long championed musical-comedy dancing that was emotionally dynamic and visually lyrical, though in *Journey to the Center of the Theater*, he would eventually deplore the choreographers who were responsible for stage characters who wondered "just who and what they were."

Bernstein could not be so waspish about Howard Taubman's comments which, though praising Robbins and the vitality of Lawrence, Kert, and Rivera, had only qualified approval for the score and no admiration for the show's mode. Taubman charged in the *New York Times* that the show was "afflicted by the problem of how to mediate the claims of the lyric theatre with those of sound commercial procedure." Pointing to "Gee, Officer Krupke," he objected to the spectacle of "little ruffians" relating their experience of mordant gang life with "a good cheer that would be suitable in a comic scene of a conventional musical show." Then looking at the bedroom scene and its brief interlude of anguished ecstasy, Taubman lamented the score's lacklustre lyricism, and concluded: "When *West Side Story* is explosive with movement, as it is a good deal of the time, Mr. Bernstein adds to the excitement with his music. When it reaches down into the human predicament of these twisted, bewildered kids as gangs or individuals, the music is unhappily neutral." In short, he remarked, *West Side Story* faltered between the two camps of musical play and opera. Many years later, in his book *The Making of the American Theatre*, Taubman returned to the heart of the matter: "To equate the conflict between races and nationalities with the romantic theme of a doomed love was to me a species of theatrical sentimentality. The problem was too serious for superficial and flamboyant parallels." In effect, Taubman seemed to be echoing Eric Bentley's criticism of the simplistic and sentimental mode of the Broadway musical — a mode that worked against the genre's ever becoming a major art form.

The carping critics are often forgotten in the wake of *West Side Story*'s eventual success, and they are mentioned here for two reasons: to show that the production was not an instantaneous hit, and to reveal that a legend was created despite certain negative facts. Stephen Sondheim contends: "The show, specifically, was not one that people wanted to see. It was a big hit with theater people but not with audiences."

The show was never sold out for long stretches — not usually more than a couple of weeks at a time. It received no boost from the 1958 Tony Awards, where its only acting nominations were for Lawrence, Kert, and Rivera, and its only awards for Scenic Design (Oliver Smith) and Choreography (Jerome Robbins). It suffered the ignominy of losing the Best Musical honour to Meredith Willson's *The Music Man*, a pleasantly rowdy and sentimental, moralistic comedy, set in a small town and guaranteed to please all those who sought family entertainment and a triumph of traditional values.

The Musical Triumphant

THE SHOW — or rather Stephen Sondheim — received notoriety when three days after the New York opening, Howard A. Rusk, M.D., published an article in the *New York Times* repeating *La Prensa*'s accusation that some of the lyrics hit below the belt as far as Puerto Ricans were concerned. Dr. Rusk wrote: "Even before *West Side Story* opened, many Puerto Ricans in New York and in the Commonwealth of Puerto Rico objected strenuously to certain parts of the new hit. The objections, however, were not so much to the depiction of the lives of Puerto Rican juvenile delinquents in New York City and their warfare with a rival gang. Rather, they centered primarily on one line of a song that referred to Puerto Rico as 'island of tropic breezes . . . island of tropic diseases.' " Then reviewing the tropical diseases in Puerto Rico of the previous month, he triumphantly proclaimed that there were "no cases of cholera, dengue, filariasis, typhus or yellow fever and only one new case of leprosy." He concluded: "Mr. Sondheim's lyrics will probably remain unchanged and Puerto Rico's morbidity and mortality rates will continue to decline. In the meantime, *West Side Story* is a dramatic and effective production and Puerto Rico is a healthy island. Would that we in New York City could find as effective measures to control our social blight of juvenile delinquency as Puerto Rico, island of tropical breezes, has found in controlling its 'tropical diseases.' "

Sondheim's lyrics could not now be ignored, although Dr. Rusk's interest in them was hardly based on musicology.

As audiences dwindled after only a little more than a year's run, the producers instituted a discount ticket policy (a two-for-one deal) and booked the show for a national tour. It was a business error, for as Sondheim says: "Hal didn't realize what a large audience there would be once ticket prices were reduced, so he made the mistake of booking a tour too early and the last couple of months you couldn't get into the theater." But it was too late to change plans and stay in New York. The tour lasted less than a year, with business being very good on the West Coast but disappointing in Chicago. As Prince remarked in *Contradictions*: "Chicago is generally disappointing with Broadway touring shows. It supports it local theatre. 'Second City blues' I think accounts for some of it. That and the fact that the quality of touring productions had been inferior for so many years."

A more profitable venture was the original cast album (recorded on Columbia js 32603) which clearly revealed the show's emphasis on youth and energy. When Bernstein and Sondheim had initially tried to sell the album idea to Columbia, they were met by a singular lack of enthusiasm. Columbia thought that nobody could possibly sing this score: it was too depressing, had too many tritones, too many words in the lyrics, and a tune such as "Maria" was too far-ranging in its notes. They turned the project down at first, but eventually reversed this decision. This turned out to be a fortunate stroke of luck for Columbia, as well as the producers of *West Side Story*, for the album became a runaway hit, in spite of being less a singer's album than was usually the case with a Broadway sound-track. As Kurt Gänzl asserts, "pure vocal ability was given less consideration than usual," with only three featured players (Larry Kert, Carol Lawrence, and Chita Rivera) required to "stretch their voices over an extended vocal line." Kert and Lawrence sounded unpretentious: he was earnest and clear, and she was quiet and delicate in her sweet soprano. Both seemed to be extending the dialogue into song rather than performing a pure musical duet. Rivera, too, was impressive — especially in "America" (catalyzed by the accompaniment of Marilyn Cooper and Reri Grist) and in the dramatic duet with Lawrence, "A Boy Like That." Gänzl rated the album one of the ten "Essential Records," along with the cast albums of *South Pacific*, *The Sound of Music*, *My Fair Lady*, *Kiss Me, Kate*, *Guys and Dolls*, *Kismet*, *Candide*, *The Music Man*, and *St. Louis Woman*.

The financial ledger thickened when the show invaded the West

End of London in December, 1958, opening at Her Majesty's Theatre to great advance publicity, primarily thanks to interest in the American cast album, which many an Englishman had contrived to buy on the black market for as much as $15. Marlys Watters, a Kansas native, and Fulbright winner, with experience in opera and oratorio, played Maria, while Don McKay, who had sung and danced with Terry Moore and Judy Garland, as well as appearing in other musicals on Broadway, was Tony. Ken Le Roy gave the English a chance to see his Bernardo, and Tony Mordente (Rivera's husband by now) repeated his Broadway A-rab. There was a new Riff in George Chakiris, slim and darkly handsome, who managed to invest the role with a lithe menace without resembling Mickey Calin, who had gone off to Hollywood westerns.

The chorus was impressive, despite being (in Kenneth Tynan's view) "too kempt" and "too pretty" and not Bronx enough. Critics recognized that this show had little to do with the Edwardian artificiality that still conditioned many of their own musicals. Tynan called *West Side Story* "the king of the [asphalt] jungle" and though he faulted Robbins' over-stylization, he praised Bernstein's score ("as smooth and savage as a cobra") and the choreography which projected the show "as a rampaging ballet, with bodies flying through the air as if shot from guns, leaping, shrieking, and somersaulting," while finding room for "a peaceful dream-sequence, full of that hankering for a golden age that runs right through American musicals, in which both gangs imagine a paradise where they can touch hands in love, without fear or loss of face." Angus Wilson wrote in *The Observer*: "This is a show, it seems to me, where predominantly the chorus matters," and he applauded the dancers for their ability to survive the "genteel freeze-up" of the two leads. Chita Rivera had the undisputed acting and dancing triumph of the show as she enhanced the nervily expressive, rawly thrilling choreography.

The critics generally vied with one another to find adjectives for their enthusiasm. "The whole has the sort of intense, concentrated, immediate impact that one gets from some such popular opera as *Carmen* when one hears it for the first time," enthused T.C. Worsley in the *Financial Times*, adding: "This is the best musical I have ever seen; indeed it gives a new perspective to the term 'musical.' " Cecil Wilson of the *Daily Mail* reported that the show "struck London last night like a flash of lightning set to music, the most dynamic, dramatic, operatic, balletic and acrobatic of all these epics from Broadway." The *Daily Express* devoted a half page to its notice along with picture coverage, and its review began: "This great musical show begins a new age in the theatre" — a view repeated with stronger sentiments by show columnist Edward Goring who claimed that *West Side Story* had a punch "like a knuckle duster" with which it "knocked spots off *My Fair Lady*." The normally sedate critics cast off their glowing fondness for *My Fair Lady*, the show that had recently had them marvelling at the exquisite culmination of an established style. Indeed, in the annual *Evening Standard* Awards, the judging panel (which consisted of film producer Sir Michael Balcon, RADA principal John Fernald, critic Philip Hope-Wallace, conductor Sir Malcolm Sargent, and critic Milton Shulman) voted *West Side Story* the Best Musical by a narrow margin of 3–2. Furthermore, the London drama critics concurred with the choice, awarding additional awards to Chita Rivera (who tied with Elizabeth Seal of *Irma La Douce* for Best Lead Actress) and to Jerome Robbins as Best Director.

Owing to union regulations, English players had to be substituted for American at the end of six months, but even at that, English audiences patronized the show in an implicit recognition of its innovative form. Harold Prince thought it ironic that, in New York, the critics had attributed the success of the show mainly to its dancing, whereas in London, audiences saw it as a great teamwork show, with a good book, wonderful lyrics, fine dancing, and worthy acting.

Back in New York in April, 1960 (with Bernstein conducting only the opening night), the show received a much better reception from critics and audiences. As Prince observed with some irony: "This time around the book was special, Sondheim was credited, and the show had a place in history. Further, they implied they had felt that way about it the first time around. But they hadn't." The revival lasted six months and 249 performances. It might have played longer, were it not for a dispute between Prince and the musicians' union. Prior to all this, sixty-five members of the touring Bolshoi Ballet attended a matinée performance on Broadway in April, 1959, and then went backstage, asking questions and offering congratulations, with Isaac Jofe of the Sol Hurok office serving as translator. They found the musical very expressive and urged Carol Lawrence to show them a few steps of the choreography. She was taken aback, but Victor Smirnov raised her above his shoulders in a classic ballet lift. Then Natasha Taborko, a ten-year veteran of the Bolshoi, gamely tried a mambo in homage to what she claimed could never be found in the Soviet Union. Soon there was a spontaneous contest of dances and leaps between the two companies. When the Russians outleaped and outwhirled the *West Side Story* cast, the latter promptly resorted to rock 'n' roll to redress the situation.

Pleased by the visitors' effusive compliments, Prince was eager to add Moscow to his itinerary of an international touring company, but he was stalled by State Department pressure. Washington was afraid that the Soviets would politically exploit the show's grim picture of slum life and gang violence. But Prince reacted sharply, as reported in the *New York Times* on June 21, 1959: "I think it is a pussy-footing policy. True, there is the risk that the Russians might do what the State Department says. But it is also possible that *West Side Story* would triumph, nevertheless." Washington forgot that Russia had its own delinquents, gangs, and violence. The Russians were determined that the show play in their country one way or another, and in December, 1959, they bruited the appalling idea (through Alexander Kuznetsov, their Deputy Culture Minister) of performing the play without dances and in a translation undertaken by the Vakhtangov Theatre. Broadway reacted with a mixture of bemusement and alarm, but the show's producers had no legal recourse because there was no copyright agreement between the U.S. and the U.S.S.R.

Any potential or actual losses in foreign royalties were more than offset by United Artists, who bought the movie rights to the musical. The *New York Times* reported in May, 1959, that Marlon Brando was anxious to play Tony but was worried whether at his age of thirty-four this would seem plausible on the screen. As it transpired, the musical was filmed without Brando, and with a far less talented actor in the role. Richard Beymer, who seemed to have nothing to recommend him as actor or singer, starred opposite Natalie Wood (pretty, stirringly emotional, but no singer), Rita Moreno (sultry, a passable singer, and a wonderful dancer), and George Chakiris (a holdover from the London production and a striking dancer). Beymer and Wood were dubbed, and Hollywood once again revealed its gross insensitivity to the integrity of a Broadway musical.

Although Jerome Robbins was signed to recreate his choreography and to serve as codirector with Robert Wise, he was let go because he was taking too much time with his meticulous rehearsals. He had been given ten weeks of rehearsal time, and experienced members of the show's New York and London companies had been recruited. Others were drawn from Hollywood, all eager to submit to the master choreographer's rigorous, uncompromising demands. George Chakiris (moving from his stage role of Riff to the screen role of Bernardo) solidly admired Robbins and is quoted in *Inside Oscar*: "Working with Robbins was the greatest experience I've ever had, because it was Jerry who first showed me how a dancer could express himself in dancing rhythms and how an actor could intensify his dramatic performance with the graceful, expressive body movements of a dancer."

Robbins wrestled with certain aesthetic questions long before the cameras started to roll. Robert Wise and art director Boris Leven decided upon what they called "dramatized realism," and they felt that the exciting dance prologue could be shot on location in the heart of Manhattan. Oliver Smith's boldly abstract sets would not work on film because they would seem "arty" and unreal. So, West 68th Street was selected — it no longer exists, having made way for the Lincoln Center revival project — but Robbins discovered that his original stage choreography did not transfer easily in such a context. "The first sequence of ballet movement," he commented, "took only fifteen seconds on the stage. The same basic idea took forty-five seconds in the movie. Why? Getting the movie audience to accept our particular frame of reference." In his view, it would require more screen time to seduce an audience, to get it to adjust to the atmosphere and to focus on just what he wanted it to see.

Robbins did not become a slave to movie techniques (such as camera angles, matching make-ups, or perfect sound), but he was well aware of the demands of the film medium. The danger in filming dances was a tendency to isolate a dance section from the story. This would not happen on stage, where the whole picture was always present. However, if he isolated steps on the screen, he would lose the point of it all. The essence of *West Side Story* was the story. The steps in themselves were less important than this. So what he tried to do was to get *over* the story *behind* the steps, as he commented to Walter Terry in the *New York Herald Tribune*. His stage instinct for accidental discoveries was exciting but antithetical to the spirit of movie making, which virtually required a draftsman's sense of pre-planning and calculation. He was obviously not bothered about Hollywood's deadlines and costs, and when he also took it upon himself to direct the actors at one point, he was deemed too expensive and difficult for the studio's good. However, he did manage to film most of the important dances, and his name stayed on the credits as co-director and choreographer.

The film was originally supposed to be "a little black and white picture," as associate producer, Saul Chaplin, promised, but it became big and stereophonic by the time the filming ended. And one of the most prized elements of the Broadway show — Leonard Bernstein's score — was turned into a blaring, sometimes grotesque distortion. What made this all the more surprising was the fact that the movie score was conducted by Johnny Green, a much-honoured film conductor who also happened to be one of Bernstein's friends.

According to Michael Freedland, "Lenny had been particularly grateful for the way Green had performed not just the Symphonic Dances from *West Side Story* in Los Angeles, but in particular the Symphonic Rhapsody from *On the Waterfront*." His trust in Green had resulted in a brilliant performance, so there was reason to expect equally good things from Green's film effort. He well knew that Green would have to develop some of the score to cope with the special needs of the screen: the Prologue, for instance, would have to be expanded to allow for a screen exposition about the rival gangs, and other numbers would have to be rethought and rescored. Bernstein had written for a maximum of twenty-five musicians in the stage pit, but the film score sometimes required as many as seventy musicians for the stereophonic soundtrack.

Green was proud of his own contribution and planned a tribute to Bernstein in advance of the movie première. Accordingly, he hosted a lavish two-part party on the West Coast. The main part was held in the Escoffier Room at the Beverly Hilton Hotel, with dessert to follow at the Green residence. Bernstein was to be treated with extravagant honour. He would be invited to hear the soundtrack on a special state-of-the-art sound system installed especially for the occasion. But the honour turned into a débacle after the dessert, coffee, and brie on crackers.

Up to this point, Bernstein was enjoying himself hugely in his characteristically expansive mode. As Green remarks, "When he laughs, he is hysterical; when he hugs you he breaks your back." The performance began with an overly ostentatious fanfare — one that Green had pulled out of the studio archives. That was loud and hyperbolic enough, but no more so than Green's recorded announcement to a captive audience that Leonard Bernstein was the greatest composer of American music in this or any other age. The tape went on: "Lenny, wherever you now are, come to me in the big room. I want you by my side at this moment." Amid the loud cheers of the milling guests, the tape added: "Ladies and gentlemen, I give you the lyrics of Stephen Sondheim and the music of Leonard Bernstein. The first performance anywhere of the soundtrack of the musical numbers from *West Side Story*." By now, Bernstein was at Green's side and was ushered courteously to a comfortable chair by the fireplace.

Then the music started, but without visuals (of even a rough cut), the score sounded grotesque. The notes seemed to be stretched out inordinately and at an unbearably high pitch.

Bernstein screamed: "Stop that goddamned machine. Whoever gave you the right to play it like that?"

An embarrassed hubbub ensued. The party turned decidedly

unfestive. The Goldwyns, William Wylers, and Billy and Audrey Wilder crept out of the house. Robert Wise did not even utter a goodnight as he left. The Mirisch brothers, who produced the film, joined the quickly departing guests. Bernstein continued to bawl at Green and at Saul Chaplin, even though Chaplin bore no responsibility for the soundtrack distortions and eventually exited in a dreadful huff.

The following morning, the Mirisch brothers summoned Green to a private meeting, where they berated him for the terrible exhibition.

Green attempted to apologize to Bernstein. When they met in the composer's suite at the Beverly Hills Hotel, Green said that the film score's tempi were dictated by Robbins, and he speculated that Bernstein would himself have never gotten along with Wise and the scenarist. But Bernstein declared: "You have betrayed my trust. You have betrayed me." Green could only retreat and apologize to the film's producers, who were beset with the expensive problem of setting things aright with a re-recording.

Bernstein did patch things up with Green and very quickly too. As Green reported to Michael Freedland, the day after Green's meeting with the Mirisches, a messenger appeared at his residence with a note from Bernstein "of such abject apology and great dignity" that "[i]t was more an explanation of his behaviour than anything. He faced what had happened with logic. It was one of the star items in my life." Accompanying the note was a pair of gold and jade cufflinks, and on the back of each was inscribed "JG — love LB." However, this formal and touching apology and demonstration of affection did not alter Bernstein's low opinion of the movie — an opinion supported by Laurents and Sondheim as well.

Filmed in technicolour and in Panavision 70 by Daniel Fapp, the movie began with an overture that was the first lurid break with the Broadway show. However, the stereophonic sound amplified the dramatic tone of the score, and the silent aerial panning from East Side, New York, to West Side accentuated the fact that this was a technically resourceful adaptation. But Robert Wise's direction frequently went for stark shocks. His prologue brought realism and abstract stylization into conflict as the two rival gangs performed their acrobatic ballet in grimy, seedy Bronx streets and alleys. The camera sometimes intruded by coming in too close to actors' make-up, showing up the Sharks' greasy, tanned faces, for instance; sometimes it stressed its own artifice, as in an aerial shot of the gang scuffle before the arrival of Schrank and Krupke. Worse, certain close-ups lost dancers in a frame — as in the "Dance in the Gym" sequence, which was further marred by a fuzzily filtered look for Maria and Tony's dream ballet. The art decoration did not always suit the medium, with some hot colours obviously stressed for passion but too calculated to be scrupulously realistic. The acting ran the gamut from Richard Beymer's rather wooden and somewhat clumsy performance as Tony and the Jet girls' Hollywood Valley ensemble, to Rita Moreno's fiery Anita, Russ Tamblyn's cool, cigarette-puffing Riff, and George Chakiris' dignified Bernardo. Natalie Wood's exaggerated Puerto Rican accent worked against her natural acting ability at times, though when it counted, she used her dramatic resources as much as the script encouraged. The singing was satisfactory but never brilliant, and it was far too obvious that neither Wood nor Beymer was actually producing the sounds. Marni Nixon's beautiful vocalization had no relation to Wood's accent or timbre, and Jim Bryant's dubbing for Beymer had more power than the actor's histrionics. Even Rita Moreno had a surrogate singing voice, with Betty Wand supplying the vocals, but the dubbing in this case did not generally detract from the flair of Moreno's acting.

The best thing about the film was, unquestionably, the dances — chiefly the work of Robbins before he was unceremoniously fired by the studio. Although there was an intrinsic collision between the story's attempts to be both sharply realistic and affectingly romantic, the choreography ultimately surmounted the problem by insisting that every dramatic or comic action have its distinctive dance idiom. Thus, from the very first syncopated, finger-snapping dance a sense of dance style was created. For the mambo piece, most of the movement was concentrated in the hips, with a controlled staccato from the waist down and with curved or linear follow-through. In the flamboyant "America" number, where the Puerto Rican boys and girls took turns advancing upon and retreating from one another, the males used vertical shapes and martial body language, whereas the females had a freer body language. The two sexes, in effect, had distinctive dance phrases, but as an ensemble their contrasting idioms worked as a single whole.

The film won extravagant praise from some eminent critics. Hollis Alpert thought that the musical was "stylishly staged in fluid, semi-abstract patterns," and that Hollywood, "for all its experience in turning out musicals, had no parallels for *West Side Story*," because for one thing, "it was *more* musical than its predecessors," containing nearly twice as much music as the average Hollywood musical. Bosley Crowther felt that it was "nothing short of a cinema master-piece," and that the "pulsing persistence of rhythm all the way through the film — in the obviously organized dances . . . such as the arrogant show-offs of the Jets, that swirl through playgrounds, alleys, school gymnasiums and parking lots, and in the less conspic-uous stagings, such as that of the 'rumble' (battle) of the two kids — gives an overbeat of eloquence to the graphic realism of this film and sweeps it along, with Mr Bernstein's potent music, to the level of an operatic form." Stanley Kauffmann generously called the movie "the finest American film musical ever made, which, almost by definition, makes it the finest film musical ever made anywhere." And Kauffmann surely could not have forgotten films like *Funny Face*, *An American in Paris*, or *The King and I*, but he was so massively impressed by Robbins' choreography (with its "feeling of thrust at the audience, of gliding in and out of reality") that he minimized his criticism of the film's failings — in particular, some of the casting and the characters' lack of high tragic attitudes.

However, the film had its detractors — chief of whom were Dwight Macdonald and Pauline Kael. Macdonald cited five reasons for disliking the movie: 1) it was in the "romantic-schmaltz tradition of musical shows — *Oklahoma!*, *South Pacific* — rather than the good one, that of *Pal Joey* and *Kiss Me, Kate*, which debunks romance and is lively and disrespectful"; 2) Bernstein's music was "pastiche," with echoes of Rodgers, Kern, Porter, Romberg, even Stravinsky; 3) Stephen Sondheim's lyrics were uninspiring ("Tonight" sounded like

"White Christmas"); 4) the romanticization of the street gangs resulted in dishonesty; and 5) the artistic problem of modulating between stylization and realism led to a discordant non-resolution, because the film makers "wanted to have it both ways." Although appreciative of Jerome Robbins' choreography and his "perfectionism," Macdonald felt that the gang ballets and dances ("the mimic world") sometimes clashed awkwardly with the "real world."

A more acidulous review came from Pauline Kael, who reacted with fulsome hostility to what she believed were expensive pretensions. Ticking off every possible flaw she could find, right from the "blast of stereophonic music" that opened the movie and the "painfully old-fashioned and mawkish" dialogue, to the characterizations (where the good characters were "innocent and sweet" and the others merely "rather comic and foolish"), the dancing ("it's trying so hard to be great it isn't even good"), the music, and even the final credits-as-graffiti. There was simply nothing she liked about this "piece of cinematic technology."

In purely technical terms, she was often on solid ground: it is true that the racial composition of the gangs was trivialized by hair dye and make-up; it is true that Bernstein's score "abandons Gershwin" for the lush romanticism of Tony and Maria, where it "begins to echo Richard Rodgers, Rudolf Friml, and Victor Herbert"; and it is perfectly fair criticism when Kael dismisses the kindly old Jewish pharmacist's "prophetic cant" or the "synthetic mysticism" in Tony's first utterances to Maria.

But when Kael equated "great American musical tradition" with "the light satire, the high spirits, the giddy romance, the low comedy, and the unpretentiously stylized dancing of men like Fred Astaire and the younger Gene Kelly," she was betraying an old-fashioned bias that failed to recognize the scrupulous artifice behind Astaire's and Kelly's apparently exuberant spontaneity. It is a well-known axiom that it is an art to conceal art, but not all art rests on camouflage. There are numerous instances when art makes a virtue of its self-awareness, and in this film's case, there was little attempt to mask some of the blatant anti-realistic devices. And so, the banality of subject matter and setting often remained oppressive, though the achievement of the movie, admittedly less so than that of the stage version, lay in the transcendence of the banal, through the jet-propelled ballets, the signature dance idioms, the clever symphonic composition. The movie was, undoubtedly, a Hollywood vulgarization, where some of the dances did, indeed, lose freshness in their rehearsed exuberance, but as Hollywood musicals go, this film was a vivid (though flawed) example of artistic integration.

The film won big audiences and many prizes. The New York film critics selected it as Best Picture of the year over such contenders as *The Hustler, Judgment at Nuremberg, Breakfast at Tiffany's, Fanny*, and *The Guns of Navarone*. And at the Academy Awards, Hollywood's annual extravaganza of self-congratulation, the movie almost swept the trophies, winning for Best Supporting Actor (George Chakiris), Supporting Actress (Rita Moreno), Cinematography (Daniel L. Fapp), Art and Set Decoration (Boris Leven and Victor A. Gangelin), Sound, Scoring (Saul Chaplin, Johnny Green, Sid Ramin and Irwin Kostal), Editing (Thomas Stanford), Costume Design (Irene Sharaff), Direction (Wise and Robbins), and Picture. Neither Robbins nor Wise mentioned each other in their acceptance speeches, but Robbins did not need to remain bitter, for the Academy presented him with an additional honour — a special Oscar for his "brilliant achievements in the art of choreography on film."

Finale

CERTAINLY, *West Side Story* was a "concept musical," having deliberately set out to tell its story by movement throughout, from the
dance "Prologue" to the mimed "Finale," and there was no attempt
on its part to separate one mode (dance, music, dialogue, acting,
lighting, décor) from another, or to allow one to dominate over
another. But the music transcended everything else, not simply
because Laurents' libretto was thin and bound to age, but because
Bernstein's score had such variety, cleverness, and power as to make
West Side Story, in the words of Martin Gottfried, "a watershed
musical." Distinctively American — right from the Copland influence to the Latin colorations and blues sound — the score remains
impressive. Of course, many of Bernstein's musical elements were
also heard in abundance in *Candide*, his earlier ambitious failure, but
in *West Side Story* these elements were so well integrated with the
plot, characters, and themes as to power the drama. The musical was
not an ethnic curiosity and not a morality play. It aimed at heart and
mind by using story material and theatrical components to express
a melancholy drama. Whether or not *West Side Story* is true musical
tragedy depends, of course, on one's conception of tragedy, but the
inescapable fact is that this work aspired to a level far higher than
that of the usual Broadway musical.

Jerome Robbins' dances, from beginning to end of the show, never
pretended to be pure, finite activities enclosed in their own vocabularies. All the dances were prompted by real life, and the dancers
suggested the hoodlum, the clown, the athlete, the villain, and the
doomed hero and heroine by more than simple signature poses. The
dances never made the mistake of developing more action than the
music could hold, and they were not stackable units, assembled on

demand without much reference to the music. (In the movie version, alas, many of them have a packaged look, as the dancers keep dancing for visual effect rather than to advance the story.) They contained inner mechanisms for expansion and contrast, and they turned the music into emotion, sometimes expressed by economic movement of a shoulder, hip, or head within a small dance area, and sometimes involving the whole body in bursts of activity.

Another landmark for *West Side Story* was in its peculiar fate on Broadway. It originally opened to a mixed reception from the major New York critics, winning only one rave. It seemed fated to be liked *and* disliked for some wrong reasons. Bernstein won due praise; Laurents was largely faulted; Sondheim was ignored. Everybody praised the dancing. Perhaps the musical was ahead of its time — and not simply because of its stark dramatic narrative.

The mid-fifties were a period of what Harold Taubman calls "the Musical Triumphant" — an era of the warmly nostalgic *The Boy Friend*, the charmingly inventive *Peter Pan*, the wickedly satiric *Damn Yankees*, the sentimentally comic *The Most Happy Fella*, and the unpretentiously conventional *Bells Are Ringing*. Certainly, there was *Candide*, but that was a flawed, overreaching musical which played only 73 performances before being put away for almost two decades. And there was, indisputably, the crown jewel of Broadway in *My Fair Lady*, but that was hardly in the true American grain, and in any case it was musical comedy — a much more manageable and popular genre than musical tragedy. In general, then, the big hits were rehearsals of old conventions and talents, and had their eyes on the pop charts as much as on box-office returns. But *West Side Story* tried for speed in acting, velocity in dancing, and emotion in singing. It was a rare instance of a Broadway musical where the visual emphasis was on youth, and where vocal ability was given less consideration than usual. As theatre chroniclers have pointed out, only the three featured players, Larry Kert, Carol Lawrence, and Chita Rivera, were required to sing over an extended vocal line. Otherwise, the males and females in the rival gangs were selected for personality and dance ability so that they would project youthful freshness and audacity.

The original production was a smash at every performance in its out-of-town previews — except for Chicago — but although it racked up $700,000 in advance sales on Broadway and ran 732 performances at the Winter Garden, it needed to be taken off and then remounted in 1960 before its quality truly registered with the critics, and then, too, only after a national tour and a London production in 1958. What helped, as well, was the popular success of the music. One irony has never faded: although the musical had been billed as a show conceived, directed, and choreographed by Jerome Robbins, it has become known as Leonard Bernstein's biggest Broadway success and one inconceivable without his score. Indeed, Robbins' striking choreography is now less widely remembered than is Bernstein's score. We tend to hear the music today without necessarily thinking of the dances. It is, perhaps, an unfair fate, for dancing can not be memorized by the public as music can be.

In an important sense, then, this book is offered as a document to offset the popular elevation of Bernstein's music to the detriment of all other elements in the Broadway production. Although much of the show seems naive today — tastes and conventions have changed since the late-fifties — it should not be forgotten that *West Side Story* was a marvel on its début, and it was especially so because it did not seek to make any single theatrical element the most important feature. Time has been generous to Bernstein's music — though there have been carping critics on this point, as well — but time has been a little careless about the impulse of the show's creators to make a single, seamless piece of art. Arthur Laurents' script is concise, spare, sardonic, and tender. It provokes music and movement, leaving opportunities for the story to be carried farther without benefit of words. The sociology and psychology are dated and thin, but the story, in its whole, artful blending of narrative, music, dance, and acting, projects a savage, embattled restlessness, an achingly romantic tenderness, and, finally, an impressive quietude. It is doubtful that without *West Side Story* there could have been later, grittier musicals on even more provocative subjects than rival gangs.

Appendix: PRODUCTION NOTES

West Side Story was first presented by Robert E. Griffith and Harold Prince (by arrangement with Roger L. Stevens) at the Winter Garden Theatre, New York, on September 26, 1957. The cast was as follows:

THE JETS

Riff (*the leader*), *Mickey Calin*
Tony (*his friend*), *Larry Kert*
Action, *Eddie Roll*
A-rab, *Tony Mordente*
Baby John, *David Winters*
Snowboy, *Grover Dale*
Big Deal, *Martin Charnin*
Diesel, *Hank Brunjes*
Gee-Tar, *Tommy Abbott*
Mouthpiece, *Frank Green*
Tiger, *Lowell Harris*

THEIR GIRLS

Graziella, *Wilma Curley*
Velma, *Carole D'Andrea*
Minnie, *Nanette Rosen*
Clarice, *Marilyn D'Honau*
Pauline, *Julie Oser*
Anybodys, *Lee Becker*

THE SHARKS

Bernardo (*the leader*), *Ken Le Roy*
Maria (*his sister*), *Carol Lawrence*
Anita (*his girl*), *Chita Rivera*
Chino (*his friend*), *Jamie Sanchez*

Pepe, *George Marcy*
Indio, *Noel Schwartz*
Luis, *Al De Sio*
Anxious, *Gene Gavin*
Nibbles, *Ronnie Lee*
Juano, *Jay Norman*
Toro, *Erne Castaldo*
Moose, *Jack Murray*

THEIR GIRLS
Rosalia, *Marilyn Cooper*
Consuelo, *Reri Grist*
Teresita, *Carmen Guiterrez*
Francisca, *Elizabeth Taylor*
Estella, *Lynn Ross*
Margarita, *Liane Plane*

THE ADULTS
Doc, *Art Smith*
Schrank, *Arch Johnson*
Krupke, *William Bramley*
Glad Hand, *John Harkins*

ENTIRE PRODUCTION DIRECTED AND
CHOREOGRAPHED BY *Jerome Robbins*
SCENIC PRODUCTION BY *Oliver Smith*
COSTUMES DESIGNED BY *Irene Sharaff*
LIGHTING BY *Jean Rosenthal*
MUSICAL DIRECTION BY *Max Goberman*
ORCHESTRATIONS BY *Leonard Bernstein*
with *Sid Ramin* and *Irwin Kostal*
CO-CHOREOGRAPHER: *Peter Gennaro*
PRODUCTION ASSOCIATE: *Sylvia Drulie*

WORKS CONSULTED

Alpert, Hollis. *Broadway! 125 Years of Musical Theatre*. New York: Little, Brown, 1991.

Amberg, George. *Ballet in America: The Emergence of an American Art*. New York: Mentor, 1951.

Aston, Frank. "Love and Hate Make Beauty." *New York World-Telegram and The Sun* 27 Sept. 1957.

Atkinson, Brooks. "Musical Is Back." *New York Times* 28 Apr. 1960.

———. "The Jungles of the City." *New York Times* 27 Sept. 1957.

Au, Susan. *Ballet & Modern Dance*. London: Thames and Hudson, 1988.

Barclay, Charlotte. "Lighting a Show Is a Man-Sized Job — For a Woman." *New York Herald Tribune* 16 Apr. 1950.

Barnes, Clive. "Clive Barnes on Jerome Robbins and *West Side Story*." *Dance and Dancers* Mar. 1962: 14–17.

———. "A New Look at *West Side Story*." *New York Times* 1 Sept. 1968.

Beckerman, Bernard, and Howard Siegman, eds. *On Stage: Selected Theater Reviews from The New York Times 1920–1970*. New York: Arno, 1973.

Bentley, Eric. *The Playwright As Thinker: A Study of Drama in Modern Times*. New York: Harcourt, 1967.

Bernstein, Leonard. *Findings*. New York: Simon, 1982.

———. *The Joy of Music*. New York: Simon, 1963.

Bolton, Whitney. "*West Side Story* Bold, Enchanting." *Morning Telegram* [New York] 28 Sept. 1957.

Bordman, Gerald. *American Musical Theatre*. New York: Oxford UP, 1986.

Boroff, David. "Preparing *West Side Story*." *Dance Magazine* 31: 8 (Aug. 1957): 14–19.

Brown, John Russell. *Shakespeare's Plays In Performance*. Harmondsworth: Penguin, 1969.

Carthew, Anthony. "*West Side* Wows 'Em." *Daily Herald* 13 Dec. 1958.

Chapman, John. "*West Side Story* a Splendid and Super-Modern Musical Drama." *Daily News* 27 Sept. 1957.

———. "*West Side Story* Brand New Hit." *Daily News* 28 Apr. 1960.

Cirlot, J.E. *A Dictionary of Symbols*. Trans. Jack Sage. New York: Philosophical Library, 1962.

Coe, Richard L. "*West Side* Has That Beat." *Washington Post and Times Herald* 20 Aug. 1957.

Coleman, Emily. "From Tutus to T-Shirts." *New York Times Magazine* 8 Oct. 1961: 20–21, 30–37.

Coleman, Robert. "*West Side Story* A Sensational Hit!" *Daily Mirror* 27 Sept. 1957.

Comden, Betty, and Adolph Green. "Early Story Plan for *Romeo*." Unpublished typescript. New York Public Library for the Performing Arts.

Crawford, Cheryl. *One Naked Individual: My Fifty Years in the Theatre*. Indianapolis: Bobbs-Merrill, 1977.

Denby, Edwin. *Dance Writings*. Ed. Robert Cornfield and William Mackay. New York: Knopf, 1986.

_____ . *Looking At the Dance*. New York: Popular Library, 1968.

Ellis-Fermor, Una. *The Frontiers of Drama*. London: Methuen, 1964.

Engel, Lehman. *Their Words Are Music: The Great Theatre Lyricists and Their Lyrics*. New York: Crown, 1975.

_____ . *Words with Music: The Broadway Musical Libretto*. New York: Schirmer, 1972.

Ewen, David. *Complete Book of The American Musical Theater*. New York: Holt, 1959.

Freedland, Michael. *Leonard Bernstein*. London: Harrap, 1987.

Frye, Northrop. *Northrop Frye on Shakespeare*. Markham: Fitzhenry, 1986.

Gänzl, Kurt. *The Blackwell Guide to the Musical Theatre on Record*. Oxford: Blackwell, 1990.

Gassner, John. *Dramatic Soundings: Evaluations and Retractions Culled from 30 years of Dramatic Criticism*. New York: Crown, 1968.

Gibbs, Wolcott. "Hoodlums and Heiresses." *New Yorker* 5 Oct.1957.

Gilliatt, Penelope. "The Voice of America." *Observer* 4 Mar. 1962.

Gordon, Joanne. *Art Isn't Easy: The Theater of Stephen Sondheim*. New York: Da Capo, 1992.

Gottfried, Martin. *Broadway Musicals*. New York: Abrams, 1979.

Green, Stanley. *Encyclopedia of the Musical Theatre*. New York: Da Capo, 1976.

_____ . *The World of Musical Comedy*. New York: Grosset, 1962.

Gruen, John. *The Private World of Ballet*. New York: Viking, 1975.

Guernsey, Jr., Otis L., ed. *Broadway Song & Story: Playwrights/Lyricists/ Composers Discuss Their Hits*. New York: Dodd, 1985.

_____ . *Playwrights, Lyricists, Composers on Theater.* New York: Dodd, 1974.

Herridge, Frances. "Surprise of Year: *West Side Story.*" *New York Post* 6 Jan. 1958.

Hewes, Henry. "The Cool Generation." *Saturday Review* 5 Oct. 1957: 22.

Hoffman, Marilyn. "She Illuminates Broadway." (Profile of Jean Rosenthal) *Christian Science Monitor* 21 Nov. 1967.

Ilson, Carol. *Harold Prince: From Pajama Game to Phantom of the Opera.* Ann Arbor: UMI Research, 1989.

Jackson, Arthur. *The Best Musicals: From 'Show Boat' to 'A Chorus Line.'* Foreword Clive Barnes New York: Crown, 1977.

Johnson, Harriet. "It's Bernstein's Music That Stirs Pulse Beat in *West Side Story.*" *Washington Post* 25 Aug. 1958.

Kael, Pauline. *I Lost It at the Movies.* New York: Bantam, 1966.

Kasha, Al, and Joel Hirschhorn. *Notes on Broadway: Intimate Conversations with Broadway's Greatest Songwriters.* New York: Fireside, 1987.

Kauffmann, Stanley. "West Side Glory." *Dance Magazine* Oct. 1961: 14–15.

Keating, John. "Far, Far from Verona." *Cue* 11 July 1957.

Kerr, Walter. *Journey to the Center of the Theater.* New York: Knopf, 1979.

_____ . "Sharks and Jets Battle in Dance." *New York Herald Tribune* 6 Oct. 1957.

_____ . *The Theater in Spite of Itself.* New York: Simon, 1963.

_____ . "West Side Story." *New York Herald Tribune* 27 Sept. 1957.

Kislan, Richard. *Hoofing on Broadway: A History of Show Dancing.* New York: Prentice, 1987.

Laufe, Abe. *Broadway's Greatest Musicals.* New York: Funk, 1970.

Laurents, Arthur. *West Side Story.* Ed. and introd. Stanley Richards. *Great Musicals of the American Theatre.* Vol. 1. Radnor, PA: Chilton, 1973.

Lawlor, John. "Romeo and Juliet." *Early Shakespeare.* Ed. John Russell Brown and Bernard Harris. New York: Schocken, 1966.

Lawrence, Carol. *Carol Lawrence: The Backstage Story.* New York: McGraw, 1990.

Lerner, Alan Jay. *The Musical Theatre: A Celebration.* London: Collins, 1986.

Little, Stuart W. "Half of Bolshoi Dancers Attend *West Side Story.*" *New York Herald Tribune* 30 Apr. 1959.

Macdonald, Dwight. *Dwight Macdonald On Movies.* Englewood Cliffs, NJ: Prentice, 1969.

Mahood, M.M. "Wordplay in *Romeo and Juliet.*" *Shakespeare's Tragedies: An Anthology of Modern Criticism.* Ed. Laurence Lerner. Harmondsworth: Penguin, 1963.

McClain, John. "Music Magnificent in Overwhelming Hit." *New York Journal American* 27 Sept. 1957.

_____ . "Really Rates All the Raves." *New York Journal American* 28 Apr. 1960.

Mannes, Marya. "Black and White in New York." *The Listener* 9 Jan. 1958.

Mordden, Ethan. *Broadway Babies: The People Who Make the American Musical*. New York: Oxford UP, 1983.

Morley, Sheridan. *Review Copies: Plays & Players in London 1970–74*. London: Robson, 1974.

"New Musical in Manhattan." *Time* 7 Oct. 1957.

Norton, Elliot. "Hub Thrills to Vitality of *West Side Story*." *Boston Record* 15 Mar. 1960.

Osato, Sono. *Distant Dances*. New York: Knopf, 1980.

"Painting Your Mood with Light." *Sunday Mirror Magazine* 10 Apr. 1955.

Palmer, Winthrop. *Theatrical Dancing in America: The Development of the Ballet from 1900*. Second ed. New York: Barnes, 1978.

Pearson, Kenneth. "Six Lonely Men: The Birth of a Musical." *The Sunday Times* 16 Nov. 1958.

Peyser, Joan. *Bernstein: A Biography*. New York: Beech Tree, 1987.

Prince, Harold. *Contradictions: Notes on Twenty-Six Years in the Theatre*. New York: Dodd, 1974.

Robertson, Allen, and Donald Hutera. *The Dance Handbook*. Essex: Longman, 1988.

Rosenthal, Jean. "Lighting the Dance." *New York Times* 21 July 1963.

Rusk, Howard A. "The Facts Don't Rhyme: An Analysis of Irony in Lyrics Linking Puerto Rico's Breezes to Tropic Diseases." *New York Times* 29 Sept. 1957.

Sargeant, Winthrop. "Please, Darling, Bring Three to Seven." *New Yorker* 4 Feb. 1956: 33–59.

Schumach, Murray. "Talent Dragnet: Casting for *West Side Story* Caused Unusual Number of Headaches." *New York Times* 22 Sept. 1957.

Shabad, Theodore. "In Moscow, *West Side Story* Becomes Picture of Life in U.S." *New York Times* 25 June 1965.

Sharaff, Irene. *Broadway and Hollywood: Costumes Designed by Irene Sharaff*. New York: Van Nostrand, 1976. Proof copy, Leo Lerman Collection, New York Public Library for the Performing Arts.

Sheren, Paul, and Tom Sutcliffe. "Stephen Sondheim and the American Musical." *Theatre 74*. Ed. Sheridan Morley. London: Hutchinson, 1974.

Suskin, Steven. *Opening Night on Broadway*. New York: Schirmer, 1990.

Swain, Joseph P. *The Broadway Musical: A Critical and Musical Survey*. New York: Oxford UP, 1990.

Taubman, Howard. "A Foot in Each Camp: Bernstein's Score of *West Side Story* Falters Between Musical and Opera." *New York Times* 13 Oct. 1957.

————. *The Making of the American Theatre*. New York: Coward McCann, 1965.

Terry, Walter. "The *West Side* Dance Story." *New York Herald Tribune* 20 Oct. 1957.

Tynan, Kenneth. *Tynan on Theatre*. 1961. Harmondsworth: Pelican, 1964.

Violett, Ellen. "Name in Lights." *Theatre Arts* Dec. 1950: 24–7.

Wain, John. *The Living World of Shakespeare: A Playgoer's Guide*. Harmondsworth: Penguin, 1964.

Watts, Jr., Richard. "Romeo and Juliet in a Gang War." *New York Post* 27 Sept. 1957.

Whittaker, Herbert. "Exciting, Dazzling, Electrifying, Energetic West Side Story Advances Art of Musical." *Globe and Mail* 16 Nov. 1957.

Wiley, Mason, and Damien Bona. *Inside Oscar: The Unofficial History of the Academy Awards*. New York: Ballantine, 1987.

Wilk, Max. *They're Playing Our Song*. New York: Atheneum, 1973.

Wilson, Angus. "Playboys of the Western World." *The Observer* 14 Dec. 1958.

Zadan, Craig. *Sondheim & Co*. Second ed. New York: Harper, 1989.